Blessing

ENERGY

Blessing!

Tired of Feeling Tired?

ENERGY

8 Steps to Energize Your Life
from the Inside Out

Cathy Alward

outskirts
press

This book is dedicated to my husband, Randy.
Thank God that I met you
at Los Angeles International Airport,
on a 2,292-mile blind date.
You're the real deal,
The best human ever,
the kindest soul,
and I love you.
My B.

Table of Contents

Introduction

Life can be hard.

Maybe you're a young mother, exhausted and feeling over-whelmed from lack of sleep. Or a student feeling the pressure of school and 'making the grade'. You might be working a full-time job, struggling to find the right balance between career and family. You may even be a man who is sneaking a peek at this book because you feel just as exhausted as your wife. (Shhh! I won't tell anyone.) Or like me, you're an empty-nester adjusting to the new direction your life is taking. There are as many stages of life as there are people.

Over the years, I've heard comments like these from people of all ages, *"I'm so tired all the time! I'm stressed out. Life just seems to get busier, how can I learn to slow down and enjoy my life?"* These comments have come from a bank manager seated across from me at her desk, to a young mother who handed me her baby while barely holding back tears, and even salespeople at Sephora who followed me around the store to find out when my book was coming out. And *bonus*, the last few years have added an extra layer of stress onto our already complicated lives. Am I right? I mean it makes sense: When we wear the mask, we miss seeing the smiles and feeling the love. When we social distance from others, we often feel isolated and lonely. And watching the confusion in the world around us has only made life more *complicated.*

You're tired. I get it.

You long for an energy deep inside of you and that's where it has to start. *Inside of you.*

This book contains years of study and results.I was an overwhelmed college student, an exhausted young mother of three sons, a busy mom of teenagers and now, a hormonally-challenged empty-nester. *"Been there, done that, doing it."*

Over the past few years, I've discovered and taken powerful steps to create an *energized life.*

A simple life.

In this book, I'll help you to get rid of the complicated stuff that's been weighing you down in the three critical areas of your Spiritual, Mental and Physical life. And finally discover the *energy* that God has waiting for you.

Here are a few suggestions as you read:

C.S. Lewis, a former self-proclaimed atheist, and iconic author of the *Chronicles of Narnia, The Screwtape Letters and Mere Christianity,* wrote this:

> *"One of the things that surprised me when I first read the New Testament seriously was that it talked so much about a Dark Power in the universe – a mighty evil spirit who was held to be the Power behind death and disease and sin...Enemy-occupied territory – that is what this world is..."*

I refer to a very real enemy, Satan, as the *'Enemy'* throughout this book. The Enemy's power and influence in our society and throughout our lives is real. Look around. Heck, watch the evening news. This is not a Harry Potter movie or a science fiction story - there is evidence all around us of an Enemy that is influencing our lives. I don't say this to frighten you, merely to help you to be aware and on guard.

It says in Ephesians 6:12 (MSG) ..."*God is strong and he wants you strong. So, take everything the Master (God) has set out for you, well-made weapons of the best materials. And put them to use so that you will be able to stand up to everything the Devil (the Enemy) throws your way. This is no afternoon athletic contest that we'll walk away from and forget about in a couple of hours. This is for keeps, a life-or-death fight to the finish against the Devil (the Enemy) and all his angels."*

I'll give you a weapon to use against the Enemy in this book. It's powerful. And it will protect you. But the best news is that *we can and will overcome the enemy.* God wins. You can count on that.

Each chapter finishes with an opportunity for you to answer questions and pray over what you have read. As you do both of these things, I encourage you to find a quiet place to spend time and let God work in you and speak to you. Sometimes, the subject that I talk about will be a little overwhelming or too much to try to cover in one prayer. I suggest finding an excellent professional counselor, a pastor or a trusted mentor to help you walk through any healing or adjustments, spiritually and emotionally, you may need help with. I've definitely reached out for help from mentors at different times in my own life. But please say the prayers slowly and out loud - the prayer is actually like a warm hug from God and I promise, you will feel his peace.

I've included scriptures at the end of each chapter. I have used key verses to speak over my life and I've seen it change me over the past few years. Reading and speaking the Word of God is incredible. *it's life-changing and powerful.* Print out the scriptures that are relevant to you and tape them up on the mirror in your bathroom or in your car. Jesus himself responded to the attack from the Enemy with scriptures - that's how powerful scripture and the spoken word of God are.

There's a song at the end of each chapter to direct your focus back to God. You can visit my website, *cathyalward.com* to find samples of the songs to listen to and it will direct you to *Spotify*: **Energy/Cathy Alward**; or you can download the songs from *Apple Music* – for a small fee – to save to your own playlist forever.

Play the song while you read the prayer at the end of each chapter. Play it in your house, loud. Play it in your small group and sing together. Play it while you're running errands in your car. Listen to it in bed at night with your ear pods. Watch it change the atmosphere in your house, in your car and in your heart.

I understand that women, (and men) of all ages - working and not working, parents and no children, married and not married, empty nesters and retirees - will read this book... Obviously, I can't address 'each and every' life-circumstance that you may be in right now. Therefore; I encourage you to use this book as a foundation to build on, and simply use *what works* - for you and your own family. Every chapter has *principles* that will benefit followers of Christ, no matter what phase of life or economic reality you are in.

Also, I'm a huge believer in tough love, so I'm pretty bold when it comes to clarifying and illustrating the principles of God, because life's too short to *tiptoe around truth*. But truth always produces beautiful results.

I hope you understand that it's never too late for you - you may be 90 years-old or just starting out in life as a teenager – whatever your story is, this is your opportunity to ignite a life of *energy*.

Energy shares the principles and observations from the Word of God that have helped me build a foundation for *Energy* in my own life.

It's worked for me. And I will never be the same.

I hope that you use this book as a reference whenever you're feeling overwhelmed and exhausted - to help get you back on track to an *energized* life.

Just like in these beautiful verses:

I Thessalonians 5:24 (MSG) says, "*May God himself, the God who makes everything holy and whole,* **make you holy and whole, put you together – spirit, soul and body** *– and keep you fit for the coming of our master, Jesus Christ. The one who called you is completely dependable.* **If he said it, he'll do it!***"*

And Isaiah 40:29-31 (VOICE) says, "*God strengthens the weary and gives vitality to those worn down by age and care. Young people will get tired; strapping young men will stumble and fall.* **But those who trust in the Eternal One will regain their strength.** *They will soar on wings as eagles...*"

Cathy

P.S. Unless you've been living under a rock for most of your life, you've heard about Jesus Christ. I'm not talking about a religion, just to be clear. Go ahead and forget all of the different religions you've heard strange rumors about over the years: Forget the weird freak shows and fake TV evangelists with slick hair, begging for money.

I want to discuss the one and only Jesus Christ and strip it down to this: *God* loves you so much, so incredibly much, that he sent his only Son, (think about that, mom and dad) to die for you and then be raised again. Yes, this really happened, for all you skeptics out there; our history's dating system hinged on this miraculous event, and it's documented and legitimate.

Jesus Christ died to forgive you of your sins, (more about that in the book) and he died to offer you the chance to accept him and to live beyond this life, basically *forever*, (no lie). Weird to some of you but... Oh. So. Phenomenal.

If you want to be a follower of Jesus, (*not* a follower of a religion) you can simply say this prayer with me and *believe in your heart*:

"Dear Jesus,
Thank you that you love me so much. I ask you to forgive me
for all the sins I have committed; maybe a long time ago or
maybe just last night. I'm not perfect, but you are. I accept you
as my Lord and Savior. I give my life to you and I trust in you. I
choose to follow you. And now my life will never be the same.
I say this prayer in the name of Jesus Christ,
Amen"

Get ready for an adventure.
And to be changed, from the inside out.

1
Let It Go

No, dear brothers and sisters, I am still not all I should be,
but I am focusing all my energies on this one thing:
Forgetting the past and looking forward to what lies ahead,
I strain to reach the end of the race.
Philippians 3:13-14 (TLB)

Oh, what we could be
if we stopped carrying the remains of who we were?
Tyler Knott Gregson

Let the past die. Kill it if you have to.
That's the only way to become what you are meant to be.
Kylo Ren, Star Wars: The Last Jedi

I'm tired of hanging on to the past.

Years ago, I lived in a little town in Ohio and my future husband, Randy, lived all the way across the country in Southern California. We were both just 20 years old when we were fixed-up on a long-distance blind date. I know crazy, right? Three days after we met, we talked about getting married. Even crazier, but I'll tell you more about that later.

Because Randy and I lived more than two thousand miles apart, we only dated in person for about two months before we got married. Not an ideal situation. Back in the day, there wasn't Facebook or Instagram or even email. Yes, for all of the kids reading this, cell phones didn't even exist yet, so all of our communication was either long-distance phone calls or hand-written letters. The phone calls were expensive, the letters were romantic, and we were in *love*.

We got married eight months after we met and a whirlwind of activity happened in those eight months: engagement, wedding plans, lots of loved ones flying out to Ohio for the July wedding, tearful goodbyes to friends and family. Because Randy had to finish his last year of college in Portland, our honeymoon consisted of flying back to California and driving up the coast with all our worldly possessions in a U-Haul trailer hitched up to our Toyota truck.

We were in our *'honeymoon bubble of love'.*

In Portland, we moved into our little apartment. My new husband went to school full time, but he also worked at a publishing company during the day, volunteered at our church, worked in the Portland prison ministry, and served as the vice president of the small Christian college he went to, (overachiever, anyone?) I barely saw Randy the first year of our marriage. I was working at a clothing store in the mall, but I was alone most of the day. I had left all my family and friends in Ohio when I married Randy, and I didn't know one single person in our new city. After the honeymoon ended and we were settled in our apartment, the *honeymoon bubble of love burst.*

'Pop!'

I can't think of a single incident that set off my emotional roller coaster ride after the honeymoon, (it was definitely a combination of stuff), but I could feel myself sinking a little deeper every day into sadness. Maybe living in a new city without my family and friends and isolated with my new husband who I barely knew, had peeled back the false narrative of the person I had convinced myself I was?

Because I was so good at putting up a happy, carefree front while we were dating, poor Randy was dumbfounded when he saw my emotional mini-breakdowns just a few months into our marriage. I'd lash out in anger at Randy when I was feeling overwhelmed and I tried to blame him for the bad feelings I had about myself. The bottom line was, he didn't understand what was happening to me and I didn't understand it either. I was a mess.

I remember crying to him one night,
"I hate Portland - it rains all the time!" (Truth)
"I hate this lousy apartment and I miss my friends,"
"No one understands what I am going through!"
"Why did I even marry you?"

It was during this time that I discovered the incredible gift God had given me in my husband. He had and still has a gift that can make almost any relationship work, *unconditional love*. Randy listened to me. He prayed with me. He didn't leave me. And he certainly could have.

That night helped me recognize that I was *messed up*. Something wasn't 'whole' inside of me. I was *off-balance* and I needed to be healed, for myself and for Randy. But, another critical reason I needed to be healed was that we had talked about having kids, and even before I got pregnant, I felt a heavy responsibility for their lives. With all my heart, I did not want to mess up these precious little humans.

So, I had several important reasons to get healthy:
* The new, unconditional love my husband introduced me to, (honestly, I was lucky)
* The desire to raise our children in a *healthy and happy home,*
* Most mind-blowing of all, an encounter with a real God who wanted to help me to *change the story that I had accepted about myself.*

I knew that my healing would have to start with me letting go of the old story and wrong belief systems that I had lived with most of my life. The good part was that I didn't blame my husband for what was 'my own pain and for my own issues.' And additionally, the hard part was that 'I didn't get to blame my husband.' This all belonged to me and I needed to face it, on my own.

So, I looked back.

I didn't have a bad childhood; in fact, a lot of my memories are wonderful. But I believe all of us interpret pain from our childhood or even as an adult, in as many different ways as there are memories. I'm going to share with you a few of the lies that I had accepted as truth in my own life. Your story may or may not be worse than mine, but I want you to understand from my own story how subtly your past can fool you into accepting, believing and then living in a lie.

It's subtle, guys.

My memories weren't chosen

When I was a little girl, my family drove across the country in our olive-green station wagon from Ohio to California to visit our cousins and, more importantly to my five-year-old self, go to Disneyland.

I vividly remember two things about this trip: First, I rode the Matterhorn at Disneyland, and since there weren't proper restraints, because this was a *long* time ago, I climbed off my mother's lap during the fast ride and ended up down in the nose of our car by the end of the ride, trembling. It's actually ironic that I love riding roller coasters today – the bigger and faster the better.

Secondly, and without a doubt something that I will never forget, I remember our station wagon pulling off the road on the way to San Diego after seeing a crowd and flashing lights, and holding my Dad's hand as we watched a man being loaded onto a stretcher by some rescue workers in the canyon far below. The man was clothed in black.

"How did he fall"? I heard my Dad ask someone in the crowd.

"He jumped off the cliff and killed himself."

Even as a five-year-old girl, I was struck by the horror of that moment. I can still close my eyes and relive the scene in my head.

You know what? I didn't choose this memory - *it chose me.*

From the moment we're born, things happen to us, both good and bad. We are consciously, but often unconsciously, living with memory-moments that have authored the person we are today.

We all have our own stories and here's a little peek at mine...

A good girl

Never good enough

My parents were pastors of a nondenominational church in a little town in Ohio and while they were devoted to raising their six kids, (girl, boy, girl, boy, girl (that's me), boy), the church always came first. My dad had a huge personality, never forgot a name and loved his congregation with all of his heart, and our mom worked hard and took care of my brothers and sisters and myself, making sure we were fed, bathed and sitting up straight in our pew every Sunday morning; which was quite an accomplishment, to be sure.

Our church was filled with salt-of-the-earth, seriously wonderful people, but I often felt pressure to act a certain way and to perform like a 'good little pastor's kid'. Maybe, it was or it wasn't my own fault, probably a little of both, but I always seemed to struggle to feel good enough. I accepted Jesus Christ as my savior when I was a little girl, and I have precious memories of my church, but when condemnation is valued more than the love of Christ, *"Houston, we have a problem."* I'm sure some of you may not even understand what condemnation means because it's a very 'church-y' term. According to *Dictionary.com*, condemnation is defined as *"the expression of very strong disapproval, the act of condemning someone to a punishment."* So basically, that means instead of thriving in an environment of unconditional love and acceptance, because all children make mistakes *(um, hello?)*, I often felt criticism from leaders and close people in my life; as a result, I lived with a vague, inexplicable guilt. I did love so many things about growing up in our church, but because I bought into how I performed on the 'outside' of me, more than who I was 'inside' of me, it started a cycle of *perfectionism* that I've struggled with throughout my entire life. I'm sure some of you can relate when I say perfectionism, right?

Part of the problem was that I had bought into the idea of *legalism*. For those of you who don't know what legalism is, legalism is defined as *"dependence on moral law rather than on personal faith."* That means that a lot of churches looked at, and some still do look at, the *'external behavior'* of a person, instead of what was in the *heart*.

Don't get me started on the damage that legalism has done to the church. The true gospel of Christ has suffered over the centuries because of mans' insistence that we have to follow a 'particular set of rules', many made up by each denomination or the church itself.

Jesus himself said in Matthew 23:1-4 (TPT), (talking about the leaders and Pharisees):

> *"The religious scholars and the Pharisees sit on Moses'*
> *throne {a special seat in the ancient synagogues where the*
> *most respected elders of the people would sit to instruct*
> *them}, as the authorized interpreters of the Law.*
> *So listen and follow what they teach, but don't do what they*
> *do, for they tell you one thing and do another. They tie on*
> *your backs an oppressive burden of*
> *religious obligations, and insist that you carry it,*
> *but will never lift a finger to help ease your load."*

Ouch. Nailed it, Jesus

We don't become a better follower of Christ just by attending church every Sunday for an hour and not swearing or not getting tattooed or pierced in the wrong place or not smoking a cigarette or acting better than someone else, or whatever particular set of rules someone has defined for you. This is all surface stuff.

Church is and can be an amazing part of your life, but don't buy into the idea of phony religious perfection. The *"I'm better than you because my sin is different"* kind of theater that has been the downfall of so many churches and *hurt* more hurting people than *helped* hurting people.

This is a fake gospel. This is not Christ. Ever.

We're all struggling and nobody, *I mean nobody*, is perfect. Not your pastor. Not your dear Grandma Gertrude. Even Mother Theresa was not perfect. They all blew it or blow it - sometimes on a daily basis. Legalism has messed up man's perception of God for far too long. I'll talk more about the effects of *sin* and the true reason it's damaging and eventually deadly. (Hint - it's not because of what other people think about us).

My personal faith and relationship with God came in as a *distant second,* (or third or fourth) to my outward behavior and appearance to others.

So, what was the first big lie that I believed about myself? I mentally took notes and checked the box next to *'You'll never be good enough.'*

☑ Check.

Body Issues

Early on, I developed a love-hate relationship with food. Okay, it was mostly a love relationship. After school, I'd often fix myself a big bowl of ice cream covered in Hershey's chocolate syrup and whipped cream, and plant myself in front of the TV to watch cartoons and *'after-school specials about a 'chubby girl being bullied at her school'.*

I could relate.

I had a weird thing for butter, too. When I helped my mom set the table, I'd sneak bites off of the stick of the butter sitting next to the bread; I didn't even bother to butter the bread with a knife. Pretty disgusting now that I think about it. I learned to use food to feel better about myself. Junk food became a delicious escape - chips, candy or any kind of sugar. And I was already self-conscious about my chubbiness.

I remember when I was around twelve years old and I was so excited to go to summer camp with my friends. All the campers were required to get a physical and I'll never forget walking out of the doctor's office absolutely humiliated after seeing my actual weight: *135 pounds*. It may not sound like a lot to some of you, but as an eleven-year old girl who was surrounded by petite friends, I felt like an absolute cow. Before I turned in my medical slip to the camp, I secretly scribbled out 135 pounds and changed it to 97 pounds. I'm sure if anyone had noticed, they would have laughed at my pretend weight.

The question was: *Who on earth was I trying to impress?*

But wait a minute, isn't this a question that has bothered you for most of your life? Am I right? *Who are you trying to impress?* I call it the *phantom critic*. Do you have a phantom critic that shadows you and whispers into your ear on a daily basis?

"You're not good enough."

"You're too fat."

"You're different than everyone else."

"You're ..." (Fill in with your own familiar insecurities).

I'll bet you a million dollars that you've heard that same lying critical voice at different times throughout your life, just like me. In fact, you're probably way too familiar with that voice.

Oh yeah, and just about that time in my life, someone decided to start calling me *"Fatty Catty"*. Catchy name, huh? My new nickname did nothing to improve my self-esteem. In fact, hearing *"Fatty Catty"* chanted when I was at my lowest made me feel even more terrible about my still-developing and growing body.

I'm not exactly sure when, or even why, all my issues with food started. Maybe I felt neglected at times as the youngest girl in a very large family? Maybe my perfectionism started kicking in at a young age? I know, without a doubt, that I was sensitive, and I learned early in my life to fill up any emptiness that I felt inside of me with a 'comforting friend' that always made me feel better about myself.

Food.

So, what was the next big lie I accepted about myself? I checked the box next to, 'Not thin enough.'

☑ Check.

Bad Choices

My best friend came to school one day with braces and I thought she looked *so cool*. She was pretty much the exact opposite of me – petite, platinum blonde, cheerleader and popular. Me? Not so much. I was already feeling inferior to the other girls in my class and a lot of them had talked their parents into getting braces. So, I came home from school that day and begged my mom and dad to let me get braces, because my teeth were so crooked and obviously hideous. Obviously. I convinced myself that *'this is what I need to finally feel like I belong'*, and my parents very sweetly agreed to pay for my 'miracle-braces'.

Unfortunately, we lived in a small town and the elderly, *(ancient)* orthodontist used frightfully-outdated procedures. The first thing he did was to pull four teeth out of my mouth, and my teeth were *big*, so - *are you kidding me?* The braces actually ended up ruining my bite, and the whole experience was kind of a nightmare. To make matters worse, I felt guilty because my parents had spent so much money on my silly decision.

So, I hid my disappointment, and suffered from headaches and discomfort in my jaw and neck for years. In my early teens, I was often embarrassed to smile and I would hide my mouth. It was a miserable way to feel about what is supposed to be my best attribute - my smile. I paid a big price to simply fit in. (More about that decision later in the book.) This is about the time when I started my life-long struggle with being a *perfectionist*.

Another hit on my self-esteem and another lie.

☑ Check.

Fragile Innocence

When I was around eight years old, I had several intimate experiences with another child. I'm not sure of my exact age because a lot of my early memories are a bit fuzzy; but I do remember that I wasn't aware of the magnitude of what was happening to me because I was just a naïve little girl.

And naturally, because it was me, *(have you met me?)* I hid what happened to me from my parents, along with my embarrassment and confusion. I just stuffed it down inside of me, like I had done with the other hurtful milestones in my life.

Over the years, people have told me that my experiences were mild compared to what they had experienced; but what happened to me, never-the-less, damaged my fragile innocence. Because this is what our childhood innocence is - it's delicate and fragile. *Wafer thin,* in fact. I felt ashamed and it was just one more reason for me to isolate myself. I was building walls and they were being built subtly, brick-by-brick.

Guilt. Embarrassment. And shame.

☑ Check.

Under Pressure

My parents were stuck with the daunting task of trying to understand me, their sensitive daughter who often felt misunderstood in a large family of six kids. I was dramatic, *(I was the one who dressed up and put on plays for my family)* and emotional, *(I could cry on cue)* and preferred to hide in my room with a book when I felt embarrassed or confused, instead of talking to someone about it.

As I grew older into my teens, my behavior didn't change much. I isolated myself when I faced the challenges of becoming a woman. The truth is, instead of turning to my parents or anyone else when I felt alone, I ignorantly chose to shut down communication and as a result, I often felt misunderstood. It was a cycle of hurt feelings and then hiding from my hurt feelings. Over and over and over.

When I was a freshman in high school, even though I fiercely protested leaving my public school of eight years, I attended the new school that had just been started at our church. There were six people in my class – talk about *living under a microscope*. I didn't have much 'breathing room' to be a normal teenage girl.

When I went away to college after graduating, I still struggled with old guilt and never really felt good enough. The *perfectionist monster* reared its ugly head, so I got really skinny one year and then I gained weight the following year. I dated a few different guys, but I was never satisfied with anyone. Looking back now, I know it was because I was never satisfied with myself. It's crystal-clear to me now as I look back on my younger years, that my 'sensitivity' definitely influenced some of the memories from my childhood. But no matter how bad or not so bad my memories were, my checklist of 'everything that was wrong with me' was written intrinsically on my heart.

And my checklist was a constant reminder that I was not enough.

I had given this self-imposed checklist permission to influence me as an adult, so that the interpretation of my past, *no matter how subtle,* was damaging my well-being as a young woman. I was a ticking time-bomb ready to explode, just waiting to blame my emptiness and insecurities on someone or something.

I had given this self-imposed checklist permission to influence me as an adult, so that the interpretation of my past, no matter how subtle, was damaging my well-being as a young woman

The Accuser

The idea of not being enough is an ancient and a well-devised plan of the enemy. It's not from God - in fact, it's the opposite of God.

In Genesis 2, the enemy, looking like a serpent because he's capable of taking on many forms, *(and still does)* approached Eve and convinced her to eat from the Tree of the Knowledge of Good and Evil. This was one of two things that God had asked Adam and Eve not to do, *(solid choice, guys),* and immediately after eating the forbidden fruit, they felt shame and had to search for some fig leaves to cover them up and hide their nakedness. Precisely what the enemy wanted. Look carefully at the two things that happened to them.

1.) They immediately felt shame.
2.) And they felt like they were *not enough* the way God had made them.

Did you know that the name 'Devil' means *slanderer or false accuser* and the name 'Satan' means *adversary*? So, the enemy knows the exact buttons to push from your childhood and your past to bring conflict into your life today. And far too often, those buttons are complete lies or half-truths concocted to make you feel bad about yourself. While my button may have been 'never feeling good enough', (by the way, this button is extremely common among women), your button may be fear or anxiety, or feeling neglected or memories of abuse in a far worse way than I experienced. There are a million buttons. I bet you thought of your button right away? Am I right?

Whatever way you have been tormented, believe me when I say, it's because you have an enemy whose purpose is to make you feel ashamed, to bring false accusations against you and to make you feel like you're not good enough.

The enemy is devious and crafty.

Shame comes in many shapes

Many of you have painful moments from your childhood, those moments that end up defining you as an adult. Think of it: If love and hugs are so important, even vital to the development of an infant, that same level of long-lasting consequence surely must apply to an improper touch, harsh criticism, or any form of emotional, mental, or physical abuse.

Dr. Martin H. Teicher, associate professor of Psychiatry at Harvard Medical School, says:

"Physical, sexual and psychological trauma in childhood may lead to psychiatric difficulties that show up in childhood {and} adulthood. The victim's anger, shame and despair can be directed inward to spawn symptoms such as depression, anxiety...or directed outward as aggression, impulsiveness, delinquency, hyperactivity and substance abuse."[1]

---

1   Martin H. Teicher, M.D., Ph.D., *Wounds that Time Won't Heal: The Neurobiology of Child Abuse*, Dana.org, *1/1/00*

So, the result is that many times the hurtful things that you may have experienced as a child causes you to respond childishly and inappropriately in all kinds of situations as an adult.

Beverly Engel, a noted psychotherapist, noted:

"Former victims of child abuse are typically changed by the experience, not only because they were traumatized, but because they feel a loss of innocence and dignity and they carry forward a heavy burden of shame. Emotional, physical, and sexual child abuse can so overwhelm a victim with shame that it actually comes to <u>define the person</u>, keeping them from his or her full potential. It can cause a victim both to remain fixed at the age he was at the time of his victimization and to repeat the abuse over and over in his lifetime."[2]

In other words, any situation that reminds you of your pain can cause you to *react* as if you were still that little five-year old child. Or a nine-year old. Or a fifteen-year old. You continue to react as if you were the same age when your offense or abuse first occurred. Sadly, this leaves many of us emotionally paralyzed as we get older. And our shame ends up *defining us.*

If you were always teased or called nasty names as a child, (like 'Fatty Catty') you may still struggle to feel good about yourself or you may never feel beautiful. Never quite good enough. Or if you were sexually or physically abused, you may find it nearly impossible to have a healthy, trusting relationship. Healthy relationships are foreign to you and unnatural. It's why your relationships often end too quickly or continue to be dysfunctional. Maybe you heard constant criticism from a parent and that critical voice still haunts you in your head as an adult? That phantom voice taunts you whenever you attempt to change your career or to even try something new. Or, maybe it was a random, unspeakable circumstance that has left you traumatized for years.

I see you, beautiful soul.

---

2 Beverly Engel, *Healing the Shame of Childhood Abuse Through Self-Compassion, Psychology Today.com, 1/15/2015*

But How Can I Forget?

Joyce Meyer, a famous motivational Christian speaker, told the world that her own father abused her for many years:

"I was sexually, mentally, emotionally, and verbally abused by my father as far back as I can remember until I left home at the age of eighteen."

By her father.

It was a tragedy, yet God pulled her out of her devastation and healed her. She says it herself:

"You may be wondering, Joyce, where was God in all this? He was there. He didn't get me out of the situation when I was a child, but he did give me the strength to get through it. It's true my father abused me and didn't love me and protect me the way he should have, and at times it seemed no one would ever help me and it would never end. But God always had a plan for my life and he has redeemed me. He has taken what the Enemy {Satan} meant for harm and turned it into something good…I am living proof that nothing is too hard for God. And no matter what you've been through or how bad you hurt, there is hope!"[3]

Hope. I am seriously in love with that word.

I know you're probably wondering, *"Why would a good God ever allow something so horrible to happen to her?"* I've often wondered the same thing. This question is one of the most difficult things to understand about God, am I right? And it's this question that mistakenly and tragically causes a lot of people to reject the choice to follow Jesus. They give up on the goodness of God without understanding the fatality of their choice.

Even though God loves us, we still live in a world of fallen and sinful people and it all points back to the Garden of Eden, yet again. Did you know Adam and Eve were created with the gift of free will? But why did God give them free will at all? Why didn't he create all

---

3   *Life Beyond Abuse,* Joyce Meyer.org

of us to just obey him? In a short answer to a complex question, God gave humans free will and the right to choose, because he didn't want to create 'robots' who were forced to love him. He wanted his creation to have the *choice* to love him or reject him. Adam and Eve could have *chosen* to live a life of freedom and communion with God, *(delighting in an exquisite and lavish garden, with every desire satisfied - sounds amazing to me)*, but they were lied to by the Enemy, *(that old snake)* who influenced them to make a choice to open up their lives to sin. An enormously stupid mistake. Their fateful choice destined *us,* their descendants, to live in a broken, sinful world.

And because we're surrounded by brokenness, we live with the result of the actions of sinful people who are capable of profoundly affecting us.

If you haven't lined up your belief system with what God says, I can say without hesitation, that you are missing out on the best life God has planned for you

The Miracle of letting go

News flash: If you're looking for a safe bubble in this life like our *Honeymoon Bubble of Love*, a place where you will never be offended, it simply does not exist. Period. If you are alive, *(which I'm guessing you are)* than you will be hurt by someone: From your parent who neglected you, to your child who rejects you or to your husband who has an affair. As you're reading this, you may be facing a betrayal, a rejection or going through a divorce that is so painful that you're not sure when – *or if* - you'll ever heal again. It's raw and stinging and your world has been turned upside down.

Recently, a close friend who was going through a divorce came and stayed with me and I witnessed one of the hardest things anyone can ever go through. She had faced a shocking betrayal after many years of marriage, her husband had shut down any hope of reconciliation and her life was going to be changed forever.

I had just finished Energy, so we sat together in my living room in our comfiest sweats and in front of a warm fire and I read this book out loud to her. She listened. She interrupted me when something challenged or provoked a memory in her. We both cried. I knew instinctively that she desperately needed to open up and talk about what had happened and she did. She genuinely acknowledged the mistakes that she had made in her marriage. She needed me, a friend, to comfort her and listen to her story, but she needed much more than merely a friend.

She needed the healing power of God's love.

Towards the end of the book and after hours of crying and praying together, she made a fundamental decision to open the door to unleash the healing love of God. What was that decision? Before God could step in to her life and begin to heal, before God could restore her, she had to come to the place in her heart where she could say these three words, *"I Forgive You"*. To her husband. Not to him personally, because he hadn't asked for her forgiveness, but she spoke the words out loud and inside her heart, to the memory and familiar picture in her mind of the man she had been in relationship with for all those years. To the very one who had betrayed her. It was, without a doubt, one of the hardest things she ever had to do. I laid my hands on her head and I prayed over her life.

But the *supernatural seed of healing* was planted when she uttered those three small words. I saw my dear friend plant a tiny seed and I've watched this seed slowly - very slowly - begin to blossom over the past months. It's like a new-found joy has bloomed inside of her heart. And that bloom is gorgeous. Because what the enemy meant to destroy, God turned into something completely new and precious for my beautiful friend.

Without any doubt or hesitation, I say to you emphatically - *only God can make you whole again*. Not your friends, not your bitterness, not re-hashing the nightmare over and over again in your head. Through forgiveness, God will slowly and faithfully lead you into his truth, anointing your head with soothing and fragrant oil and he will fill your cup, a cup that you thought would be empty forever, with his healing grace. Again, and again. And when you feel empty tomorrow, because you sometimes will, he will faithfully fill it again. And the seed planted in your heart will be watered by God's healing grace and you will eventually *bloom*.

I believe it with all my heart.

Forgiveness releases healing. It is the fundamental reason Jesus came to die on the cross, because Jesus is the *'essence of forgiveness'*. When you miss this profound truth, you tend to reject Jesus and *his best* for you and, oh boy, as you'll discover later in this book, is his best better than your best. He loves you and wants you to experience a healthy life, but profoundly, your healthy life will only begin with forgiving. And letting it go.

When I was a young wife, I sat down with a trusted mentor and shared offenses from my childhood that I knew I needed to forgive. Maybe most of them were very small in comparison to other people, but a few were significantly critical to my own healing. *I knew they were critical because they were powerful enough to influence my well-being and joy.* In fact, that's your 'barometer' to use: If it is important enough to affect your life today, it's important enough to forgive or be forgiven. Period. You don't owe anyone an explanation of why something is so important to you.

I wrote down the memories that I knew had offended me, and I walked through each one separately and forgave each person who I felt had sinned against me or offended me.

I'm not suggesting that you try to dig up each and every old or silly offense – life happens. People will always be capable of accidently offending you because, well, we're all human. I'm talking about that one time that has been bugging you your entire life. I'm referring to the offenses that occurred during a vulnerable time in your life that have traumatized you and have probably left you lying awake at night, hurting and confused. I think you know exactly what I'm talking about.

In my own walk towards forgiveness, certain events that were not necessarily something I needed to forgive – like legalism or even religion – resulted in a revelation of God's grace.

If you're a new Christian, or even if you've known Christ for many years, we all have adjustments we are compelled to make as we understand; the depth of the love of God, the grace and truth of the gospel, all rolled into one. So, as I've studied the Bible for myself, I've been careful to allow God to change me and adjust any wrong attitudes or belief systems that may have not lined up with the truth of the Gospel. In fact, our 'false mindset or belief system' is exactly what most of this book is about. If what we believe does not line up with what God says, we are wrong. Always. In fact, if you haven't lined up your belief system with what God says, I can say without hesitation, that you are missing out on the best life God has planned for you.

I think all of us need to be sensitive to God revealing himself to us in different ways throughout our lives, because we simply can't box God in. When you allow God to change you and speak to you throughout your life, you open up your heart to healing on a deeper level. You open yourself up to possibility and miracles and peace. (Stay with me throughout this book. His energy is waiting when you line yourself up with his truth and it is truly amazing.)

Back to forgiveness. I spoke with a few people, whom I was *aware* that I had hurt many years ago, to ask if they would forgive me as well. Obviously, I had probably hurt people without being aware of it, but I truly felt like a weight had been lifted off of my life many years ago. Of course, I've since been offended and I've no doubt hurt others at different times over the years, but since my first encounter with forgiveness as a young woman, I've learned that it's so much easier to forgive quickly, to ask forgiveness if I know I've offended someone, and to walk in freedom.

To let it go as quickly as possible.

The Fight to be Free

How do you know what sin is as a new Christian?

In James 4:17 (AMP), it says: *"So any person who knows what is right to do but does not do it, to him it is sin."*

Another way to put it is, *'sin is missing the mark'*.

The word 'sin' in the Greek actually means 'to *miss the bullseye.'* I believe that the 'bullseye' is the life that God has meant for you to live to your full potential.

> *They suddenly recognize that God is a living, personal presence, not a piece of chiseled stone. And when God is* **personally present**, *a living Spirit, that old, constricting legislation is recognized as obsolete.* **We're free of it!** *All of us!*
>
> II Corinthians 3:17 (MSG)

God wants you to listen to that still, small voice, (sometimes not so still and small), that lets you know when you are going to mess up *before* you mess up. That voice is there if you listen. It makes you feel uncomfortable when you're about to miss the mark and you'll feel *convicted*, not condemned. How do you tell the difference between conviction and condemnation? God's voice, *conviction*, calms you, leads you, reassures you and brings comfort. Always. *Condemnation,* or often the enemy's voice, brings fear, confusion, discouragement and worry; It's usually loud and obnoxious.

God's spirit in you is your spiritual conscience. God gives you that quiet voice, a living Spirit inside of you, *(it sounds a little 'woo-woo' to some, but it should be reassuring; it's better than the alternative),* to help you make the right decisions throughout your day when you're tempted or distracted.

You want the truth? Sin always involves making a *stupid choice*, in the moment, because it feels good. In the moment. But it always, always has consequences. We pay for those choices. Sin offends God. but even more critical to all of us, sin messes up your life. Especially as an adult. It's ugly, dark and *it never ends well.*

About ten years ago, I was friends with a guy who was not my husband. I was so caught up joking around and having fun, that I ignored the damage that this friendship could have had on my marriage. It was only an emotional friendship, but it could have possibly gone the wrong way physically, mostly because I didn't have 'wise boundaries' set up around our friendship. I convinced myself, *"Oh, he's just a friend, you're fine, you're not doing anything bad"*, but I was playing with fire. Through a series of God-ordained, (I'm positive) events, I stopped all contact with this man.

Now, you might be thinking, *"Come on, Cathy, you didn't do anything that bad!"* But my husband and I knew that to make our marriage indestructible, we had to maintain absolute transparency with each other in our marriage. I asked my husband to forgive me and he did.

And since that very moment that he forgave me, my husband has continued to trust me to be a better woman, to be a Godly example and allowed me to walk in the freedom of forgiveness. Our marriage has continued to grow stronger, day by day. He's my best friend on this earth, without a doubt.

But, one of the most powerful decisions that we have made in our marriage - for many years now - is that we do not *bring up each other's past mistakes*. Period. Oh sure, we'll sometimes bring up a little annoyance that bothers us or a silly problem that we remind each other to deal with, but the big stuff? Never. We try our best to use Jesus as our example and forgive and *forget* our past slip-ups. Of course, neither of us are perfect and I'm not arrogant enough to claim that we'll never make a mistake, but I *am convinced* that grace and forgiveness is a powerful path to walk in. Grace is now peacefully present in our everyday life, and authentic, honest freedom surrounds us.

If forgiveness from your loved ones did not happen for you, I am so, so sorry. But even if your loved ones or another person in your life didn't forgive you, Jesus is always waiting to forgive and love you. He is.

But God's love and forgiveness can heal and soothe your pain. It is, without a doubt, that powerful.

God's grace always seems to startle the religious

In John 8:1-11, the story is told of a woman who was caught in the act of adultery. The religious leaders dragged her in front of Jesus one day, accusing and judging her.

Jesus, his heart filled with compassion, bent down on his knees and started writing in the dirt. Some people speculate about what he was writing, but I personally think that he was writing down the sins of the religious leaders. I also think that when they saw what he was writing, they felt convicted of their own sins and felt ashamed. *What about the beam in your own eye, right?*

Jesus said, *"Let's have the man who has never had a sinful desire throw the first stone at her."* Ouch. They had nothing left to say. They left Jesus, one by one, and the woman was left standing alone.

Jesus said, *"Dear woman, where are your accusers? Is there no one here to condemn you?"*

The dear woman said, *"I see no one, Lord."*

"Then I don't condemn you either," Jesus remarkably said, *"Go, and from now on, be free from a life of sin."*

Be free.

Jesus encourages you to 'embrace forgiveness', either from God or give it to another. Forgiveness is a gift that allows you to be free, both in the giving and receiving of it. God's grace is real and it's beautiful.

Accept his grace.

> He **forgives** your sins – every one. He heals your diseases –
> every one.
> He redeems you from hell – saves your life!
> He crowns you with love and mercy – a paradise crown.
> He wraps you in goodness – beauty eternal.
> He renews your youth –
> you're always young in his presence.
> Psalm 103:3-5 (MSG)

"You're always young in his presence." What a beautiful thought.

Hurt People, Hurt People

Wow, is this a true statement. You probably never know the *history* behind someone who hurt you. Even if what they did was just a little offense; or if it was tragically, something far worse. I love the TV show, *"This is Us,"* because we get to see everyone when they were younger and it helps us understand 'why they do what they do'; what their story is. Why do you think this show usually moves us to tears? Because it tells the story of each person, and explains, not justifies – a

clear distinction – their story. To this day, I know that judging someone will never make me feel better about myself, because what I see
someone else struggling with today could very easily be the thing I
struggle with on another day.

Or if someone hurt you, maybe you can try to see the person
who hurt you as a young child? They were innocent at one time in
their life. We all were. Somehow, they lost that innocence and they
themselves were never healed. If you can take the courageous stand
of seeing them in a different light, hopefully, it can help to soften the
pain. This doesn't excuse them of their behavior. Ever. This more importantly allows you to stop the continuation of pain inside of you.

> *You may have to declare your forgiveness*
> *a hundred times the first day and the second day,*
> *but the third day will be less and each day after,*
> *until one day you will realize that you have forgiven*
> *completely.*
> *And then one day you will pray for his wholeness*
> *and give him over to me,*
> *so that my love will burn from his life*
> *every vestige of corruption.*
> — William P. Young, <u>The Shack</u>

Healing warmth

> **Bless** *those who curse you,* **pray** *for those who abuse you.*
> Luke 6:28 (ESV)

The act of forgiving someone is powerful, but the real freedom
lies in praying for them and sending them love. This step is often forgotten when you forgive, but it may be even more powerful.

It's been raining, (no surprise in the Northwest) and getting colder
this week and I feel winter just around the corner. Today, while I was
writing upstairs in my office, I was *freezing*. In spite of being dressed
in flannel pants, a sweatshirt and fluffy slippers, I couldn't seem to get
warm. So, I went downstairs and filled up my bathtub with steaming
hot water; even though hot water is supposed to dry me up like an
old prune, I risked it. I gingerly slid into the hot water and slowly felt

my body warm up. It was the only way to get rid of the bone-chilling cold I felt.

That warm bathtub reminds me of the love of God. If we use his love as the basis for everything we do, the warmth of healing is incredible.

The old nagging pain will slowly fade, with love and forgiveness, just like the old newspaper clippings I keep from important events throughout the years in my keepsake box: They're yellow and tattered and musty. They've lost their importance.

My mistakes are old news. Your mistakes are old news. The mistakes that others have made toward you and I are old news.

Old news.

This is your moment to let it go. Your brilliant future is so much more important than your musty past. Please don't waste another minute, because forgiveness unlocks your future. Let it go and be free. The Father is waiting with open arms.

Are you ready to let it go?

Steps to Forgive:

First, when I was a young wife, I sat down with a trusted mentor and shared my past from my childhood that I knew I needed to forgive. I wrote down all the relevant painful memories that have bothered me, maybe for years, and I walked through each one separately and forgave at that moment each person that had sinned or offended me; one at a time. I pictured looking into their eyes as I forgave them.

It didn't mean I would never remember those memories any more. It was a symbolic act of laying them down at the feet of Jesus and walking away from that particular pain.

Second, I walked through any forgiveness I needed to ask God for.

Third, I did go to a few different people who I thought I had offended from my past. Look, everybody messes up. If you feel like you don't than *you are part of the problem.* Don't be too proud to get it right.

You know what? In the process of learning to ask forgiveness and even to forgive others, you learn an incredible gift that I'll talk about in another chapter: Humbleness. This is one of the greatest gifts you will ever discover. It is literally worth gold.

In my most important relationship, my husband and I have almost made it a game when we argue. Each of us tries to be the first one to say, *"I'm sorry. I messed up. Please forgive me."* It's funny, the more you learn to say *"I was wrong, please forgive me"*, the easier it becomes to continue with your amazing life. How many marriages would have been saved if husbands and wives had learned to say *"I'm sorry"* quicker? How many times has our pride got in the way of walking in peace and forgiveness? Sadly, too many times.

And finally, I sent the ones I forgave *or asked to forgive me, love.* I literally said, Send _____ your love, God." And my healing began.

Take Action:

(Please use a separate piece of paper for the list below)

1) What are the painful offenses or hurtful circumstances that have caused you to either have bitterness toward someone, or to even believe a lie about yourself from your past? Who do you need to forgive?

_____

_____

_____

2) Is there anyone that you have hurt that you may need to ask for forgiveness? (I know God will only bring to mind what is necessary. We're human. Accept the truth, but try not to fabricate circumstances. If you feel like you need to contact them to ask for forgiveness, that's up to you, you'll know.)

_____

_____

_____

3) Is there anything from your past or even from last night that you know you need to ask God to forgive you for?

_____

_____

_____

4) Choose a verse to print out that inspires you about forgiveness, (choose one from this chapter or find your own), to remind you to choose to forgive. Always.

_____

_____

_____

After you have gone through the forgiveness prayer, please take the time to destroy your notes in this chapter. Your notes are meant for your eyes only and I promise you will never forget the day that you decided to forgive and accept forgiveness.

Prayer:

Please say this prayer out loud

Dear God,

Thank you for loving me, and for sending your son, Jesus Christ, to forgive my sins.

I don't want to be stuck in my painful past any longer.

First, I ask you to help me forgive the people who have offended me on my list: (Read from your notes)

Second, I ask you to forgive me for the mistakes or sins I've made that don't line up with your will for my life. I don't want to miss the mark: (Read from your notes)

Lastly, I pray that you will bless those who have hurt me, or who I have hurt. Send your love to each of them: (Mention each of them by name)

Thank you for being a God of new beginnings, full of grace and mercy. I want to have a fresh start, so I can live my life without bitterness.

Because I am so much more than my past, I let it go.

In the name of Jesus,
Amen

Energy Playlist:
O Come to the Altar

Energy Verses

So **repent** {change your inner self – your old way of
thinking, regret past sins} and **return** {to God – **seek His
purpose for your life**}.
So that **your sins may be wiped away** {blotted out,
completely erased},
so that **times of refreshing** may come from
the presence of the Lord
{**restoring you** like a cool wind on a hot day};
Acts 3:19 (AMP)

Continually **pursue peace with everyone**, and the
sanctification without which no one will {ever} see the Lord.
See to it that no one falls short of God's grace;
that **no root of resentment springs up**
and causes trouble, and by it many be defiled;
Hebrews 12:14-15 (AMP)

…Many are the sorrows and frustrations
of those who don't come clean with God.
But when you **trust in the Lord for forgiveness**,
his **wrap-around love** will surround you.
Psalm 32:10 (TPT)

Hatred stirs up quarrels,
but **love makes up for all offenses.**
Proverbs 10:12 (NLT)

When someone becomes a Christian, he becomes a
brand new person inside. He is not the same anymore.
A new life has begun!
II Corinthians 5:17 (TLB)

No, dear brothers, I am still not all I should be,
*but I am bringing **all my energies** to bear on this one thing:*
Forgetting the past and looking forward to what lies ahead,
I strain to reach the end of the race and receive
the prize for which
God is calling us up to heaven
because of what Christ Jesus did for us.
Philippians 3:13-14 (TLB)

Energy starts with Forgiveness

2

No Fear

For God has not given us the spirit of fear ...
2 Timothy 1:7 (NKJV)

It's impossible to disappear from you
or to ask the darkness to hide me, for your presence is
everywhere,
bringing light into the night.
There is no such thing as darkness with you...
Psalm 139:11-12 (TPT)

Now, because of you, Lord,
I will lie down in peace and sleep comes at once,
for no matter what happens,
I will live unafraid!
Psalm 4:8 (TPT)

I'm tired of being afraid.

I come from a long line of hotel-lovers. Give me a cushy king-size bed, a clean bathroom and room service and I'll be happy as a clam. But when Randy and I were first married, we were broke, and living on

Ramen noodles and love, so camping was the next best thing to a hotel for us. I remember one Friday night, years ago, we packed up our tent and sleeping bags and headed out for a weekend of camping. It was late by the time we got to the campground and all the campsites were taken, so the manager of the place kindly directed us to another place to stay a few miles away. When we drove up to the campground, it was almost dark and kind of creepy, and it seemed like we were the only other campers around. Randy and I set up our tent, *(it was comical)* and started a fire to roast hotdogs for dinner. After we finished eating, it was too dark to see anything, and even creepier at this point, so we zipped up our tent and climbed into our sleeping bags. *(Yeah, that zipper on our tent really helped me feel more secure.)*

I was almost asleep, when suddenly, twigs snapped outside.

My eyes flew open. The moon was bright and I saw shadows moving across the outside of our tent.

Shadows.

Okay, this felt like a bad movie. My husband was snoring, loud and obliviously, next to me. I poked him and whispered in his ear, *"Randy, I think there's someone outside!*

Wake up!"

As we laid huddled together listening to the bizarre noises, I imagined every possible scenario. Remember the scary ghost story from junior high sleepovers about the 'mental asylum escapee with the hook', scraping across the top of the victim's car, or in this case, tent? *Yep, so did I.* The noises continued, and I was positive we were next in line to become Big Foot's 'dinner'; or dessert from the sound of it.

I finally couldn't take it anymore.

"Randy", I whispered urgently, *"don't you think you should go check it out or something?"*

It didn't dawn on me that if he went outside and got eaten by whatever was out there, I would still be left in a flimsy Walmart tent with a zipper for protection. But my hero-husband put on his tennis shoes and grabbed a large flashlight, the only thing remotely close to a weapon that we had, pulled the zipper open and crawled out into the dark. Finally, after what seemed like an eternity, I heard him laughing. What?

"It's cows, Cath!" he yelled from outside, "It's just a bunch of cows!" We were completely surrounded on every side of our tent by a large herd of cows. Munching away on the grass. I could deal with cows, but 'holy cow', *(bad joke)* did I imagine some creepy scenarios.

Shadows

Like the shadows on our tent that night, isn't it crazy how our minds can easily become obsessed with the *what-ifs* of life? Back when we were first married, it was easy for me to worry about the *what-ifs* – we had just bought and built our new home, had our first baby, and within a few weeks of moving into our house, Randy lost his job. *Yikes.* We could barely pay our mortgage, besides all the other bills, which left Randy scrambling to find another job. This definitely wasn't in our master plan and it was a scary time for us. The shadow of *what-ifs* consumed me: *What if we can't afford to live in our beautiful new home? What if Randy can't find another job? What if we lose everything? How are we going to pay for college for our new baby when we only have 18 years to save?*

The last sentence was meant to be funny, but let's be honest, how often do you let your mind wander and make something way worse than it really is? Fear can pop up at any time of life. It doesn't matter if you're a young college student, a wife or momma, or an empty nester.

Fast forward to today. I am an empty nester. For almost 24 years, we raised our three sons in a beautiful little beach town in Southern California. They grew up surfing and our whole family adored the ocean and the near-constant sunshine. It was darn-near perfect. Then, my dear husband had the brilliant idea to move to the Northwest. Back to Portland. What was he thinking?

So, several years ago we left California and moved back up to Portland to start a new venture for our business. Honestly? I felt lost. It's like everything hit me all at once in Portland. The rain. *Again.* No more going to the beach any time I wanted. Our boys were all grown up and gone, *(spoiler alert: for those of you with darling little tykes, you have no idea how hard this is.)* I missed my friends. I was dealing with my crazy hormones and I felt lonely.

But do you know what I felt more than anything? I felt uncomfortable. Why did I feel so uncomfortable? Let me explain.

Several years ago, I knew, *I just knew* that I was supposed to write a book about my story and what God had shown me about balance and finding energy. I told a lot of people about the book and I got some awesome feedback. Anyone else would have been encouraged, but nope; I found ways to avoid writing. I was an expert at coming up with excuses to put off writing this book. In Portland, and then Washington, I got my real estate license *and I couldn't possibly find the time to write.* We moved twice, and built a house for a year; *no way could I find the time to write.* We were on the road a lot, *and I could never find time to write.* I made a lot of excuses, but the truth was, I was afraid of how silly I would look if I put the book out there and it failed. I kept asking myself, *"What if I look like an idiot? What if this, what if that?"* I was just plain afraid.

But, in spite of my fears, I couldn't get rid of the feeling that this was the next step God wanted me to take in my life. I knew that I would feel uncomfortable until I just made myself sit down at my little desk and finish. I'm not kidding - the uneasiness I felt in bed at night staring at the ceiling in the dark was way worse than working through the fear and putting myself out there with this book.

I learned a big lesson. God often makes us feel unsettled and uncomfortable when he's trying to push us to walk towards a new goal or in a different direction. And to me, the uncomfortable feeling that only God can use to motivate us to take a bold step is worse than the fear of failing.

How about you? Have you been putting off something because you're just plain scared? Maybe you're afraid of looking like an idiot in front of your family or friends, like me. Maybe you don't feel qualified. You're embarrassed. You're only *this* or you don't have enough of *that*. We're all experts at coming up with great excuses to avoid humiliating ourselves. If you've been putting off doing something because of fear, I want to inspire you right now to take a chance; because who are you trying to impress? Probably that critic that whispers in your ear everyday of your life, like mine did and does. I'm acquainted with my own crafty, deceptive critic; very well acquainted. But we have a weapon to shut that critic down. And it's powerful.

Neon Lights

Have you ever read the Bible and felt like a verse had flashing neon lights on it? I mean **blink, blink, blink**. I was reading Proverbs 3:5-6 (TLB) and all of a sudden, these verses spoke to me exactly where I was at this time in my life. *Boom*. Listen to this:

> **Trust in the Lord completely,**
> *And do not rely on your own opinions,*
> *With all your heart rely on him to guide you,*
> *And he will lead you in every decision you make.*
> Proverbs 3:5-6 (TLB)

Okay, first of all, God wants you to *trust him*. Period.

He wants you to trust him and not to trust in your own opinions or insecurities or worries; hence, *"Don't rely on your own opinions."* Easy to say, much harder to do. Why? Because I like to be in control.

But don't you like to be in control, too? Truly, one of the hardest things for me to do is to trust. I tend to be skeptical. And I also tend to be very independent: In fact, you might as well just call me stubborn. Really, all of us usually think we can figure it out better than God can. But, really? You can figure it out better than the God who knew you before you were born?

> **You saw who you created me to be before I became me**!
> *Before I'd ever seen the light of day, the number of days you*
> *planned for me*
> *were already recorded in your book.*
> Psalm 139:16 (TPT)

Again, if you believe there is a God who created you, you have to understand and be comfortable with the assurance of this: He has a plan and his plan will be far, far better than anything you could ever plan. Far, far better, friend.

I have been testing out my trust muscles a lot lately. I've been working out these muscles by ignoring all of the other *shadows* that want to steal my peace, and repeating this verse over and over during the day, and sometimes when I wake up at night - because you can't be a passive believer in God. *You have to be aggressive with your trust.* This is so important, that I'll say it again:

"You have to be aggressive with your trust."

Trust Him.

Trust Him.

Trust Him.

Trust in God with all your heart. And when you get tired of reminding yourself, remind yourself again: *Trust God.* Because this is the only dependable and even, supernatural solution for fear.

If you believe there is a God who created you, you have to understand and be comfortable with the assurance that he has a plan; and his plan will be far, far better than anything you could ever plan

Second, your understanding or the way you perceive life, is often *just plain wrong.* You can't see the whole picture of your life, so how on earth can you trust your own feelings to guide you? I can't tell you how many times I've been embarrassed or felt afraid to do something and looking back, I realized how silly my fears were. I mean, do we really need to worry about what some old friends from high school think about us? Or even our coworkers, or dear old Aunt Sally? Who the heck cares? Repeat after me, *"Who cares?"* Listen to this:

That is why we can say without doubt or fear,
"The Lord is my Helper, and
I am not afraid of anything that mere man can do to me."
Hebrews 13:6 (TLB)

As long as what you do is in line with God's purpose for your life, what does it matter what people think? (*I'll talk about your purpose in a later chapter.*)

Third, we can learn to recognize God in the midst of our life and see the little miracles that happen every day, because they do.

While I was finishing this book, it was clear to me that I couldn't do this without God. I reminded myself constantly that God alone is my source. I acknowledged his unique plan for my life and just kept putting one foot in front of the other, or in my case, just kept writing one word after another. I memorized Proverbs 3:5-6 and I repeated it over and over. I probably said it dozens of times a day and still sometimes do. It wasn't the only verses I repeated, but they're some of the most important verses of my life. What's ironic is that Proverbs 3:5-6 has always been Randy's life verses. I always knew they were, but those verses had never spoken to me quite as powerfully as they did that one day when I needed to hear from God. That's how powerful the revelation of the word of God can be. Those verses literally catapulted me into finishing this book.

My Favorite Verb

Years ago, we were on a family ski trip to Colorado when our boys were very young. The snow had been falling heavily that day and our boys begged us to let them play in the snow outside our condo with their cousins, while I got dinner ready. They promised they would stay in the front yard with their cousins, and my oldest was eleven years old at the time, so my husband and I figured that they would be fine. However; our youngest son, Chase, was just five years old. And to understand Chase, you have to know that from the day Chase was born, he was constantly on the go. It was almost impossible for him to sit still. My husband and I always told people, "*Never name your child a verb.*" Get the picture? Anyway, I agreed they could play outside as long as they kept an eye on Chase, our little verb.

After an hour or so, I called the boys in for dinner. It was still light outside. Everyone ran inside . . . except Chase. I stared at the boys. "*Where's your brother?*" Nobody had the faintest idea what had happened to him. The adults quickly threw on their coats and headed outside to search around the condo. After a few long minutes, we began to get a little frantic. Especially me. In fact, I became distraught. I was pounding on the doors around the complex and turned into 'crazy lady' pretty quickly. *Wouldn't you?*

During those brief moments, my emotions went from worry, to full-blown fear, then to imagined kidnapping plots, possible injuries, and, of course, guilt for letting him play outside in the first place.

About an hour later, we were discouraged and we came inside and finally called the police. Miraculously, they told us they had Chase at the police station, warm and safe.

The tears of relief stung in my eyes as we raced to the police station. There he was, looking very small and holding an oversized teddy bear given to him by the kind officers, which made him look even smaller. What had happened? Apparently, a man in a car had seen Chase walking on the side of the road, picked him up and drove him to the police station.

My life would never be the same. It is one of the life events that haunted my husband and me for the rest of our lives. We were terrified. All kinds of *'what-ifs'* attacked me, even after he'd been found: *What if the man who picked him up had kidnapped him? What if Chase had fallen into a deep snowdrift and suffocated? What if a car had slid into him on the side of the icy road?*

After that traumatic day, I had to decide whether or not I was going to spend the rest of my life as a chronic worrier over everyone in my family. And I could have. Since they were little, my boys all played sports, and loved snowboarding, surfing and wakeboarding. All my boys lived, (and still live) on the wild side. *Was I going to always worry while they were having fun?* We've been to the emergency room on too many occasions. *What about when they got older and could drive? Would I worry about them driving at night?* And yes, accidents did happen.

And it wasn't just worry about my kids. *Would I worry about the results of my own medical tests?* I've been called back for second and third opinions and thankfully, everything came out okay; but I was sweating bullets waiting for the results of the tests. Or *would our new business be successful up here in the Northwest?* The part of our business that we started up here actually didn't work out. But guess what? We're okay. We're still here. And now I have darling grandchildren to add to that list of worries if I let myself. The list of *'what-ifs'* for my family was, and is, never ending.

But I have learned since that very scary day that we lost Chase, to refuse to continue letting the *'what-ifs'* dominate my thinking. I refuse to waste my precious time on this earth worrying about the shadows because: It. Does. Me. No. Good. *Nada.* Nothing good ever comes from worrying. It's a pointless waste of time. I heard someone describe worrying as turning 'around and around' in a circle like you used to do when you were little. Remember when you would twirl around in circles until you got so dizzy that you could barely stand up straight? It didn't take you anywhere and it messed up your head.

Sounds a lot like worrying, right? Worrying about something, anything, is one of the biggest *energy*-drainers that we allow into our lives. You know what? Worry never makes us feel better, it never takes us anywhere, it never gives us a great idea or puts a smile on our face. Never. It's just a useless waste of moments we will never get back again.

On our annual family ski trip – Chase, the boys and Dad

Breaking News

My sweet friend, if it didn't end as well for you as the day we found Chase, I am so sorry. My heart hurts for you, because I do understand that life is so, so fragile. Listen to this scripture-reminder for all of us:

*The reality is **you have no idea where your life will take you tomorrow.** You are like a mist that appears one moment, then vanishes another. It would be best to say, "If it is the Lord's will and we live long enough, we hope to do this project or pursue this dream.* James 4:14-15 (VOICE)

Last year may be one of the most bizarre years we've ever lived through. (And if you're reading this book in the future, I'm sure you've heard your grandparents talk about it.) There was political turmoil, the entire world battled a strange virus, we prayed for racial healing and many of our cities and small businesses were burned to the ground right before our eyes.

Like a strange mist seeping through a crack beneath the door, fear crept inside our very living room. Our children were affected. Our relationships suffered. Something sinister shattered our peace. I truly believe a lot of what happened that year was a distraction to bring division and hate between all of us. I'm not sure from where, but clearly, we were forced out of our *comfort zone.*

Or were we? Maybe it forced us to *define* our comfort zone.

It's strange to me that early that year I started waking up in the middle of the night with a burden for our world. I watched scary things happening, unexplained and troublesome, but I started to pray. Sometimes I got up at two or three in the morning, on my knees, asking God to protect my family and other families. I felt an urgency I couldn't explain. And I do believe that God heard me.

But, more importantly, my time alone with God inspired me to be a *warrior* instead of a casualty of fear. Why? Because God has not given me the *spirit of fear.*

No, he has not.

This verse emboldened me: "*For God has not given us the spirit of* fear..." And I will not allow myself to live in fear. Never. Fear is just a *shadow*. Because, when you focus on fear that may be on the outside of you, you lose peace on the *inside of you*.

Please listen to this powerful verse:

Lord, even when your path takes me through
the valley of deepest darkness,
fear will never conquer me, *for you already have!*
You remain close to me and lead me through it all the way.
Your authority is my strength and my peace.
The comfort of your love **takes away my fear.**
Psalm 23:4 (TPT)

We, as followers of Jesus Christ, have been given *God's authority* as our strength and peace. His love should comfort us and take away our fear. I'm tired of listening to rumors and fear-mongers. And the evening news using 'sensationalism' to create panic. When we let fear creep into our lives – and I use the word *creep* for a reason – it begins to wrap itself around any *'what-if'* situation in our minds and we open up ourselves to fear; like the strange mist that crept into our living rooms.

I've talked a lot about shadows in this chapter, because I see shadows as being the exact opposite of what God is. *God is light.* The only shadow we should set up camp in - the only shadow that he tells us to trust in - is *his shadow.* Every other shadow is a distraction:

He who takes refuge in the shelter of the Most High
will be safe in the shadow of the Almighty.
He will say to the Eternal,
"My shelter, my mighty fortress,
My God, I place all my **trust** *in you."*
Psalm 91:1-2 (VOICE)

In the bible, it talks about the disciples of Jesus being out on a boat in the middle of the night, and a storm was raging. *(Sounds a bit like our life sometimes, am I right?)* One of them peered out into the night over the waves and saw Jesus walking towards them. Now, the bible is very *clear* about it being around four in the morning, so it was dark. And stormy. My question would be, *"How did they see Jesus walking on the water if it was dark and stormy?"* He must have been illuminated in some way because they thought he was a ghost.

Could it be because he is the 'light of the world'?

Jesus then asked Peter to walk on the water with him. *Whoa!!* This was a big ask for Peter just to trust. But even though Peter had enough faith to take a step out on the water, *(kudos, Peter);* when Peter took his eyes off of Jesus, off of the only true 'light', he began to get scared and started sinking. When he took his eyes off of the only one who could help him make it across the water, he lost his *trust*.

Jesus responded, *"What got into you, (Peter)?"* In other words, *"Why can't you just keep your eyes on me in the middle of the dark night?"* Or, *In the middle of creditors calling, in the middle of a child being sick, in the middle of betrayal, or being fired from your job, or you've just gotten a scary medical diagnosis?*

Or even in the middle of a pandemic?

In all of these 'shadowed' situations, Jesus simply asks you to keep looking at his supernatural *light,* and trust him to help you walk across the rolling waves or to get you to the next step in your journey:

And those who huddle in night, those who sit in the shadow of death,
*will be able to rise and walk in the **light**,*
*guided in the **pathway of peace**.*
Luke 1:79 (VOICE)

When we choose to keep our eyes on Jesus, on the light, he will take hold of our hand and guide us on the pathway of *peace*. We do not have to be casualties of fear. Peace is waiting on the other side of *trust in God*. I promise. You're in the safe place, *your comfort zone*, when you trust God. Trusting in God is your own personal 'comfort zone.' And this is where you can stay for the rest of your life.

Your safe place.

A Broken World

I was with my brother, Marcus, in his doctor's office the day that he was diagnosed with terminal throat cancer. He had lived an amazing life and when he died a little over a year later, he left a wife and three beautiful children behind. He was only forty-seven years old. I was devastated. Don't tell anyone, but he was my favorite brother.

So many people wondered how God could allow this to happen to such an incredible man, with so much to give back to the world? I asked my husband that very question one day at coffee after we heard about Marcus' diagnosis. My husband wisely told me, *"This world is imperfect and broken and we humans have to face the results of this imperfect world."*

Worry is just a useless waste of moments we will never get back again

But why did a perfect God allow the world to become so broken? Not just with a terrible disease like Marcus had; but golly, after watching the news every night and seeing the nosedive the world is taking all around us, doesn't it make you wonder?

Pastor Rick Warren, author of *The Purpose Driven Life*, gave a profound perspective. He wrote: *"Nothing works perfectly, because sin has damaged everything. We only need to look at the physical world around us to see this. Natural disasters and deformities are everywhere. We live on a broken planet; it's not perfect anymore… God never intended for animals and humans to have defects and deformities, breakdowns in DNA. Yet we all experience genetic issues to one degree or another.*

Nobody's body works perfectly. And we see the effects of original sin in another way — physical decay and death. Because death entered the world with sin, everything is decaying and will ultimately die. Solomon, the wisest man in the world, summed it up this way: No one can control the wind or stop his own death (Ecclesiastes 8:8).

While we deal with sadness, sorrow, suffering, difficulties, dead ends, and discouragement, keep this in mind: God is preparing a better place for us. He wants us to live forever with him in a perfect heaven where there will be no more sorrow or tears."⁴

And listen to this scripture:

*Our earthly bodies which die and decay are different from
the bodies we shall have when we come back to life again,
for they will never die.
The bodies we have now embarrass us
for they become sick and die;
but they will be full of glory when we come back to life again.
Yes, they are weak, dying bodies now,
but when we live again they will be full of strength.*
I Corinthians 15:42-43 (TLB)

How true is this? Who doesn't wish that we were still in the Garden of Eden? Or maybe that this world was a perfect Disneyland, with sparkling fairies and all the delicious frosted chocolate cake and gooey pepperoni pizza we could eat, without gaining a pound, where everyone loved each other, like 'totally', and we all lived happily together without any problems.

But it's not. Brothers die. Children are abused and neglected. Spouses betray each other. Relationships end. We're surrounded by darkness a lot of the time and our world just seems to be getting darker. But we can choose not to dwell in the darkness.

Light

Because I live in the perpetually wet Northwest, I have found myself dreaming of the sun in the middle of winter. After it's been drizzling and spitting rain for months on end, I crave the heat of the sun. I miss the endless sunshine of California. I miss my shorts and flip flops and laying out on the hot sand. It makes me smile just thinking about it; the sun just makes me feel younger. It's a source of *energy*, am I right?

---

4   *The Purpose Driven Life*, Ric Warren, 2002

It always surprises me when I talk to a store clerk or waitress, and they tell me how much they love the rain up here. I always think to myself, *"Yeah, but that's because you don't know any different. You're just used to the dark days. You've never experienced the light like I have."*

Same as God's light, when you really experience it.

God doesn't muck around in the *shadows*.

Stop following the shadows around anxiously and keep your eyes glued on the only one who can save you. Trust God.

Trust keeps you going in the right direction. It protects you. It's a quiet confidence that comes from knowing that God can always do it a million times better than you can and *he will*. I promise you with all my heart.

Keep looking up to the light and trust in God.

Trust in God.

Trust in God.

Trust is your tool to be a *warrior,* instead of a casualty of fear.

And God is your great defender.

It's going to get better, I promise. Keep reading.

Take Action:

1) What are some things (shadows) you worry about on a regular basis?

   _____

   _____

   _____

2) Do you ever have trouble sleeping or relaxing because of stress or worry? _____ If so, what are some ways you can use trust to give your worries to God before you go to sleep? (i.e. write down your worries, pray and give them back to God, talk to your spouse.)

   _____

   _____

   _____

   I often play beautiful worship music to fill my home with peace or I listen to it on my ear pods at night. Godly music is powerful and capable of dispelling fear, subduing your racing thoughts and ushering you into peace.
   A peaceful atmosphere of rest.

3) What are some steps you can take to remind yourself to stop worrying about your future and trust in God?

   _____

   _____

   _____

4) Choose a verse that inspires you to never fear and to trust God, always.

_____

_____

_____

Prayer:

Please say this prayer out loud

Dear God,

I am so grateful that you have promised me that I do not have to live with the spirit of fear and worry in my life. I understand that my life has an incredible purpose.

*Whatever happens to me or my family, I was meant to walk **boldly, with confidence** in the power and strength of Jesus Christ.*

I declare that I am a child of God and I belong to the only one, true God.

God, you have a plan for my life, and you will give me the strength I need to complete my purpose.

*Father, I give you all my fear and worry right now and I will continue to give you my fears every day. Because your mercies are new every morning, I can finally start living an energetic life. **A life full of energy and trust in you.***

In Jesus Name,
Amen

Energy Playlist:
Defender

Energy Scriptures

*For God has not given us the spirit of **fear** ...*
2 Timothy 1:7 (NKJV)

It's impossible to disappear from you
or to ask the darkness to hide me, for your presence is everywhere,
bringing light into the night.
There is no such thing as darkness with you.
Psalm 139:11-12 (TPT)

Now, because of you, Lord,
I will lie down in peace and sleep comes at once,
for no matter what happens,
I will live unafraid!
Psalm 4:8 (TPT)

Night's darkness is dissolving away as a new day of destiny dawns.
So, we must once and for all strip away what is done in the
shadows of darkness, removing it like filthy clothes.
And once and for all,
we clothe ourselves with the radiance of light as our weapon.
Romans 13:12 (TPT)

Life came into being because of him,
*for his **life is light for all humanity.***
*And this Living Expression is the **Light that bursts through gloom** –*
*the **Light that darkness could not diminish***
John 1:4-5 (TPT)

Light, space, zest-
That's God!
*So, with him on my side I'm **fearless,***
afraid of no one and nothing.
Psalm 27:1 (MSG)

Every gift God freely gives us is good and perfect,
*streaming down from the Father of **lights**,*
who shines from the heaven
***with no hidden shadow or darkness** and is never subject to change.*
James 1:17 (TPT)

Lord, even when your path takes me through the valley of deepest darkness,
***fear will never conquer me**, for you already have!*
You remain close to me and lead me through it all the way.
Your authority is my strength and my peace.
*The comfort of your love **takes away my fear**.*
Psalm 23:4 (TPT)

*This is the life-giving message we heard him share and it's still ringing in our ears. We now repeat his words to you: God is **pure light**. You will never find even a trace of darkness in him.*
I John 1:4-5 (TPT)

The word from heaven will come to us
*with **dazzling light** to shine upon those*
who live in darkness, near death's dark shadow,
*And he will **illuminate the path that leads to the way of peace**.*
Luke 1:79 (TPT)

***Perfect, absolute peace** surrounds those*
whose imaginations are consumed with you;
*they **confidently trust in you**.*
Isaiah 26:3 (TPT)

Let the dawning day bring me revelation
of your tender, unfailing love.
***Give me light for my path** and teach me,*
*for **I trust in you**.*
Psalm 143:8 (TPT)

<u>Trust in the Lord completely</u>,
And do not rely on your own opinions,
With all your heart rely on him to guide you,
And he will lead you in every decision you make.
Proverbs 3:5-6 (TLB)

Trusting God is the source of your Energy

3

Power

For God has not given us the spirit of fear, but of power…
II Timothy 1:7 (NKJV)

Everything we could ever need for life
and complete devotion to God
has already been deposited in us by his divine power.
II Peter 1:3 (TPT)

I'm energized every time I enter your heavenly sanctuary
to seek more of your power.
Psalm 63:2-4 (TPT)

And we pray that you would be energized
with all his explosive power
from the realm of his magnificent glory,
Filling you with great hope.
Colossians 1:11 (TPT)

I'm tired of feeling weak.

Believing in God is radical.

If you truly believe, it's magical. It's life-changing. Billions of people have been affected by Jesus Christ and their belief in God. It's bigger than *The Secret*. Way, way bigger. It's bigger than Oprah or Tony Robbins.

Consider with me these scenarios:

If your plane is going down and you're grasping your seat, screaming at the top of your lungs, *(probably wishing that you had eaten that warm, gooey Cinnabon at the airport before you got on the plane)*,

Or if you're sitting in your doctor's office listening to a horrible diagnosis and you only have a month to live. *Your heart is racing, you can barely breathe and the doctor is saying something, but you can't hear a word...* You will not, *I repeat,* you will not be crying out for Oprah or Tony. I promise you. Most of us will be calling out for God.

Because we all desperately look for God in the dark and frightening moments of our life. Why? Because most of us know *intuitively* that God is the only one who is capable of helping us. That he's got the power and no one else does.

Over the years, many of you have followed or maybe just been entertained by the parade of Influencers, talk show hosts, celebrities and YouTubers trying to help you find happiness or love or riches. Isn't it funny how most of the popular trends or self-described experts always end up pointing back to basic Christian principles, such as gratitude, (remember gratitude journals?) forgiveness, unconditional love, being careful what you say, and the list goes on? Like in their brilliance, they came up with these principles, without crediting God. However; unless all of their good thoughts and 'Big Magic' point to God as their *source*, their best intentions will fall to the ground, deflated and lifeless. Their opinions will be like a weathered, metallic helium balloon that sags and drifts to the ground on the side of the road in the desert.

'Fake truth' simply doesn't last long – it's achingly empty.
*For what the world says is wisdom is **actually foolishness** in God's eyes. As it is written: the cleverness of the know-it-alls becomes the trap that ensnares them. And again: The Lord sees right through the clever reasonings of the wise and knows that it's **all a sham**.*
So, don't be proud of your allegiance to any human leader,

(Sorry Oprah & Tony) *for actually, **you already have everything**!*
It has all been given for your benefit.
I Corinthians 3:19-21 (TPT)

For God intended that your faith not be established on man's wisdom
*but by **trusting** in His **almighty power**.*
I Corinthians 2:5 (TPT)

Shock and Awe

Let's take a look at this world you live in.

Do you really understand how spectacularly fine-tuned the universe is? There are hundreds and hundreds of examples of a miraculously delicate balance in this world we live in. Our universe and the earth are so fine-tuned and our own DNA, (down to the tiniest molecules and cells) is so absolutely mind-blowing, that it begs for and points to 'Intelligent Design'. Here are just a few examples:

The earth receives 99% of its energy from the sun. We are 93 million miles away from the sun. *(Apparently farther in the Pacific Northwest – I'm missing the sun as I write this.)* If we had any deviance from the 93 million miles between the earth and the sun, *the earth would not exist* as we know it. (In the words of NSYNC, "Bye, Bye, Bye")

The earth is on a 23.5% tilt. It is being balanced between the moon and the sun; if there was no moon, there would be no life on earth.

Our atmosphere is 21% oxygen; with any more or less oxygen, there would be no life on earth.

The ocean and our blood contain 3.4% salt; with any more or less than this percentage, there would be no life on planet earth.

This is called 'the science of fine-tuning', and there are hundreds and hundreds of unbelievably precise numbers that add up to life on planet earth.[5]

What about gravity?

---

5   *Everything is Spiritual Tour,* Rob Bell – 7/2012, youtube.com

Lee Strobel, a reporter and former atheist, contended, *"Right now, the force of gravity is set precisely at a certain point along this incredibly long continuum. As a result, life on Earth can flourish. But pretend the dial setting for the force of gravity were to be moved by just one single, solitary inch. Immediately, the impact on life in the universe would be catastrophic! Animals anywhere near the size of human beings would be instantly crushed, (so, humans would too) and that's just from moving the dial setting a mere inch compared to the width of the entire universe!"*[6]

To me, it's far easier to prove intelligent design than a random 'Big Bang Theory' - evolving from *nothing* into *something*? I'm not a scientist but I have bet my entire life on intelligent design. A Creator. A big God.

What about your amazing body? Skeptics of creation remind us that we share a percentage of our DNA with chimpanzees, gorillas and orangutans. That's true, but did you know that we are also genetically related to bananas, cabbage and slugs? *(I knew I bonded with banana split sundaes for a reason.)*

Speaking of DNA, if you unraveled your entire DNA, it would stretch over 10 billion miles – that's just what's in your own body. And you have over 100 trillion cells in that same body.

Simply put; you, my complex friend, are absolutely mind-blowing. That should make you smile. I am.

Your creation is first explained in the Bible. Ah, the Bible.

The Bible is the only book in history to be written over a span of about 1,500 years, (I mean, that's quite an attention span.) Over 100 million Bibles are sold each year, around the world. Over 5 billion Bibles have been sold throughout history. *(Hey, NY Times' bestsellers, the Bible has got you beat, just saying.)*

And then came Jesus Christ. All of human history was altered by the birth and resurrection of Jesus Christ. Our complete dating system was based on Jesus. 'BC' literally means *before Christ* and AD means *in the year of our Lord*. The birth of Jesus Christ made the dividing point of world history.

---

6   *The Case for a Creator: A Journalist Investigates Scientific Evidence that Points toward God*, Lee Strobel

But perhaps the greatest miracle is staring into your baby's eyes and watching in wonder, as their eyes light up for the first time; or when a precious smile brightens their face and they grasp your finger, trusting you to love them.

The incredible, beautiful and magical miracle of life.

I presented all of the evidence above to bring some shock and awe back into your life. To hopefully, shock you out of your numbness and wake you up. Because, too often we ignore the little miracles that shape our days. Take a deep breath: *The God and creator of the universe loves you and you have a deposit of power in you.*

And if you follow Christ, God has given you the ability and gift to tap into His power. It's time to claim the *energy* and power of God that belongs to you.

Divine Power

In this crazy life, we make our kids breakfast every morning, run to Target, watch marathon Netflix, pay our bills, sit at our kid's soccer games on Saturday, hate our job, wish we had a job, fight with our spouses, love our spouses, scroll on social media, get bored, laugh, cry, sometimes we get sick and all of us will eventually die. Life is moving pretty fast.

My husband and I were watching the movie *Cast Away* the other night and if you haven't seen it, it's about a time-obsessed FedEx manager who survives a plane crash in the South Pacific and finds himself marooned on a deserted island. While he's figuring out how he's going to survive on the island, he pulls his pager out of his pocket, *(obviously, this was filmed before every 12-year-old owned a cellphone)*, shakes the pager and realizes that it's completely waterlogged and has no power. It's a completely worthless piece of plastic. Your cell phone would be completely worthless, too, if you didn't plug it into a power source every time it needed to be charged. In fact, you could say that your cellphone's value depends on the battery that charges it.

This book is about finding *energy* to live your best life. In the same way that you need to charge your cellphone every day for it to work, you can't live your life the way God created you to live without plugging into his *energy*, his power on a daily basis. It truly is your own responsibility, (not your husband's, not your mom's, not your favorite Instagram influencer, or anyone else's responsibility) to give control of your life over to God and the divine energy that's been deposited in you. Listen to this:

> Be supernaturally infused with strength
> through your life-union with the Lord Jesus.
> Stand victorious with the force of his **explosive power**
> flowing in and through you.
> Ephesians 6:10-12 (TPT)

I read *explosive power* in the verse above, didn't you? His explosive power is flowing in and through you. When you plug into God with prayer, trust, *(there's that 'T' word again)* and use your faith to believe that His ways are far, far better than your ways, you tap into His power and connect to God as your life-source. How do you tap into this *power* that is available to everyone who is a follower of Jesus? The following are some ways that I've discovered to connect with God. Get ready for explosive *energy*.

Draw Close

I underestimated the power of prayer in my life. Big time. It's powerful and I've seen it work over and over in my life throughout the years. Do you remember when my son got lost in the snow that day? Did I pray and ask God to help us find him? Absolutely. And we did find him, thank the good Lord. But I am a firm believer in praying ahead, before the unknown emergencies happen.

Early in our marriage after our three sons were born, Randy was on the road a lot with a new job. He had started to be anxious about leaving his little family alone for long stretches of time and it was stressing him out. Randy was actually the program director for a men's movement called *Promise Keepers* years ago, and our company produced the music for the events. *(Anyone old enough to remember it?)* Thousands and thousands of men across the country met in their various cities at large stadiums to worship God together and pray for God to be first in their lives so they could lead their homes as Godly fathers, *(it may be time for another Promise Keepers, right?)*

One memorable night at one of the events, Randy felt impressed to get on his knees and declare that *our boys belonged to God.* He felt like God had given our boys to us as a gift and we could trust that God loved them more than we ever could. My husband dedicated our children to God. It was powerful. He felt an unexplained immediate peace that night and it stayed with Randy throughout the years. It was beyond any human understanding. When he got home and explained to me what had happened to him that night, we both prayed the same prayer together, and I too felt the same unexplained peace that Randy had experienced. I'm not kidding. For years, we have both lived with the assurance that God has each of our sons in his hands and nothing harmful will happen to them, except if allowed by God.

What a place of peace. This is an example of the impact that just one of our prayers had on a huge part of our lives: our kids. We had to recognize that God has the big picture of our lives and we don't. So many times, I've thought that I knew what would be the best for me – all the way back to when I was fixed up with my husband, Randy. How on earth would I have found this incredible man, (who lived thousands of miles away) had I been chasing after the wrong guys in college or concerned that I didn't have a serious boyfriend. I shudder to think what I might have settled for.

God knew.

Keep that in mind, all of you wonderful single people reading this. It's better to trust God, and *wait,* then to get yourself into a bad or unhealthy relationship. Guys, a great movie, some buttery-popcorn and maybe a friend to laugh with on a Friday night is so much better than being stuck in the wrong relationship. Trust me.

Better yet, trust God.

I underestimated the power of prayer in my life. Big time. It's powerful and I've seen it work over and over in my life throughout the years

So how do I pray?

> Let the **dawning day** bring me revelation
> of your tender, unfailing love.
> **Give me light for my path** and teach me,
> for **I trust in you**.
> Psalm 143:8 (TPT)

✳ First, I think there's something powerful about starting out your *morning* with God. You know why? Because throughout the night, our minds are filled with unconscious thoughts and dreams that we really can't control. How many times have you woke up in the morning and been shook up by a crazy dream? I'll talk more about unconscious thoughts in another chapter, but just remember that the morning is a prime time to focus on God.

I choose to stop all distractions. I put my phone away, *(I know this is a tough one)* and turn off the TV. I get to a quiet place. All of you have a quiet place that you can go to: Maybe it's the office in your home, maybe it's a closet, *(a little claustrophobic for me)* or maybe it's even your car parked in the garage or during a lunch break at work, *(done that)*. Even if you're a young momma and you have a gorgeous colicky baby who's been up all night; all it takes is sitting with a cup of coffee on the couch or the kitchen table, while your darling angel is finally snoozing, close your eyes and concentrate on God. No matter what phase of life you're in, you are capable of finding a quiet place for 15 minutes or more.

✳ We also need to come before God with a clean heart and mind, because he's God and we're not. Look, all of us mess up. I do pretty much daily, but I always start my time connecting with God by making sure that I ask for forgiveness for any way that I've missed the mark. *(Even if it's just that you've been in a bad mood for two days, or you're mad at your husband for yelling at you for charging too much on the credit card – been there.)*

It's helpful to know that, as you become closer with God, you become more aware of the little or big things that you've allowed to interfere with your relationship with God. It's like this: If you were out to coffee with a friend, hopefully you wouldn't go through your entire visit without taking care of any hurts or bad feelings between the two of you? I'm the kind of person who wants to get it all out and talk over any problems. I guess you could say I'm confrontational.

Be *confrontational* with God. Don't let anything get in the way of your peace. I say this a lot in this book:

It's not so much that your sins hurt God, (although I'm sure they do), it's that our *sins end up messing up or destroying our lives.* (Read that statement over and over until you feel it in your bones.)

All sin does is produce emptiness and pain and it will eventually destroy you, if you let it continue. *(Train wrecks, remember?)*

It steers you away from the best course that God has planned for you; Every. Single. Time. If not sooner, later. And when you're steered off course, you're missing the mark.

So, start your prayer time with confessing your sins. Get it right with your Father God. Ask for forgiveness. (Go back to Chapter One if you need a reminder). And if you're not sure what 'right' is, keep reading this book; and the Bible. Hang out with God and it will be obvious. Remember, he lives inside you and you can leave your heavy weights – *your sin* – at the foot of the cross. Forgiven and forgotten. Daily.

✳ There is without a doubt something powerful about saying, *"Thank you".* Tell God thank you for the breath you take or the sun that shines or the rain that falls. Tell God thank you for your beautiful child, your health or your dog or your delicious juicy In-N-Out burger with grilled onions you had for lunch. *"You can't be fearful and grateful simultaneously,"* Tony Robbins said, *"so if you want to conquer {fear}, maybe it's time to train your nervous system to go into gratitude more naturally."* Um, Tony, even though you can't save me when my plane is crashing, this is so true. Oh, and Oprah, you hit the nail on the head with the 'Grateful Journal' – such a powerful tool.

There's a reason God wants us to be grateful – it takes the focus off of what we're *missing* in our life and puts our focus on the *blessings* in our life. And being grateful has been proven to promote happiness, increase our energy levels, strengthen our heart and immune system, expand our capacity for forgiveness and decrease stress and depression. The benefits are endless.

Every time I say thank you to God for something, anything at all, it is a form of worship. It is my choice to direct my gratefulness towards God, and he responds by filling me with *contentment* and joy. It works.

✳ Very early in our marriage, I began praying over Randy and myself. Even before my kids were born, I would pray for each of them in my tummy, and I still pray for them to this day, along with their wives and our grandchildren. God has given each of us women and men the authority to pray over our homes and our families. It's so powerful. How many times have you heard someone famous say, *"I never would have made it, if my Mom (or Dad) hadn't been praying for me"*?

It's in your court now. It's your turn. You are the prayer warrior for the next generation.

For you, O Lord, bless the righteous man
{the one who is in right standing with You};
*You surround him with **favor** as with a shield.*
Psalm 5:12 (TPT)

Walking in God's *favor* is the safest place to be. Whatever you need in your life, take a deep breath and ask God to fill you with whatever it is. Here's exactly what I do: I close my eyes, say *"Fill me with your favor, God,"* take a deep breath and hold my breath, imagining the *favor* of God, for instance, filling me throughout my body. Every cell. From the top to the bottom of me. Then, I slowly exhale. I actually ask God to fill me with his love every day. Because it helps to fill any empti-ness that I sometimes still feel, because I'm human, and so are you. Or I breathe in and ask for the *joy* of God to fill me. I breathe in and ask for his *energy*. Every single time I do this, I feel strengthened. And I've witnessed him bless my life with favor, love and joy, over and over again.

Deep breathing exercises have been proven to combat anxiety and stress, so this is powerful in so many ways. In fact, I refer back to deep breathing methods a few times in this book. You can try it while you're running errands in the car, *(obviously, don't close your eyes)*, during your prayer time, or lying in bed at night. It always helps to relax you; and at the same time, God is filling you up with his power.

How cool is that? It works.

God is the shield that protects. Don't be afraid to ask for the blessings of God.

If you're single, start praying for your future and speak favor over everything you do. Pray for your future mate, if that's what you want. You can be specific, or better yet, don't be specific. I certainly never dreamed up my husband in my prayers for a future husband. I truly did not know the kind of man I needed, because I barely knew who I was at the age of 20, *(the infant-age I met Randy)*. But I did have a 'come-to-Jesus' moment when I asked God to take over my life, and that's when a lot of good stuff started happening, *(more about that later)*.

Pray and meditate on good things. I envision my family and I being *healthy, energetic, favored and blessed* for ninety-plus years. I speak and pray a hedge of protection around my entire family – protection from disease, sickness, accidents and any other attack.

And what you speak out of your mouth matters. More than you can imagine. Listen to this verse:

*Your words are **so powerful** that they will kill or give life...*
Proverbs 18:21 (TPT)

Oh boy, did you hear that? Your words are so powerful that they can *kill or give life*. You can literally *speak life* into your spouse, your kids and the different situations that you go through. In my quiet time with God, I use my words to pray. Whatever power or healing that I need in my life, I use my *words* to speak into it and pray for it:

*....the **words of the wise soothe and heal.***
Proverbs 12:18 (TPT)

Nothing is more appealing than
speaking beautiful, life-giving words.
For they release sweetness to our souls and
***inner healing** to our spirits.*
Proverbs 16:24 (TPT)

***Watch your words** and be careful what you say,*
*and **you'll be surprised how few troubles you'll have.***
Proverbs 21:23 (TPT)

Can you see how important it is to be careful with what you allow to come out of your mouth? The power of your words during your quiet time and throughout your day will have a *profound effect* on you and your family's life. I talk about the power of your words throughout this book; but for now remember that you can use your words to connect to God's *power*. The most important thing I hope you can understand is that God has the very best lined up for you, but only when you make this life-altering decision:

To let him take control of your life. And trust him.

**You will forever be chasing
counterfeit truth
if you don't decide to always,
always trust God -
And oh boy, is life exciting when you
embrace surrender and learn to trust**

Prayer changes things

I can't tell you how many times Randy has walked into the house and said, *"Have you been praying, Cath?"* Every time he's said that, something has either changed for the better, or even a miracle has happened. And we laugh. This is how God works in our lives. We are by no means perfect, but I *know* that God has heard and answered many of our prayers over the years.

Prayer is also checking in with God throughout the day. When you're running errands or standing in line at Costco or lying in bed at night – when someone or some situation pops up in your mind – often, it's time to pray. There are a million different things that each one of us can pray for. Your prayer life is your call, but here are some ideas: *Your spouse, your children, favor over your family, your future spouse, health, healing, purpose, dreams, failures, successes, joy, peace, financial blessing, laughter, job, protection over your family, your community, our nation and this world.* And, oh my goodness, does our world need prayer right now.

Take the limits off of God and pray for those things that seem impossible. Be bold enough to ask.

I pray because I'm helpless.
I pray because the need flows out of me all the time,
waking and sleeping.
It doesn't change God. It changes me.
CS Lewis

Trust and have Faith

The 'T' word again. I'm talking about it again because it is just that important.

Trusting God has to be your default in life.

That's a pretty bold statement, but it's true. You will forever be chasing 'fake, counterfeit truth' if you don't decide to always, always trust God. And, oh boy, is life exciting when you embrace surrender and learn to trust. It's like a muscle that you work out and slowly build up. And some of us have to do more squats than others; yes, for sure I always do, and squats are *so freaking hard*.

Just like trusting God. I know it's tough to trust; especially when you're sick, or the creditors are calling, or your child is struggling in school, or you and your husband are barely talking. But, the more you trust, the more you can let go of what *you think* is best and find out every day that *God's way* is just better. Period. Wait and see. How does God know a better way for every single human being alive or who has ever lived? *That's the mystery, baby.* That's the reason the Bible tells us boldly that, *"His ways are better than our ways.":*

This plan of mine is not what you would work out,
neither are my thoughts the same as yours*!*
For just as the heavens are higher than the earth,
so are my ways higher than yours, and my thoughts than yours.
Isaiah 55:8-9 (TPT)

We were created to live in wonder

Remember the 'Tree of the Knowledge of Good and Evil in the Garden of Eden'? Guess what? God asked them not to eat of that tree because it would take the mystery of life away from Adam and Eve, and in some ways, it did. But I believe it's a gift from God to live with *mystery* – because you let God take control of your life and you give Him permission to be your *North Star*, the constant, the rock, the foundation in your life.

And, it's both a relief and an adventure.

There are many times in my life, when – if God had let me direct my own path – it would have most likely been disastrous, *(that baseball player I dated in college?)* That's why I ask God to open the right doors and close the wrong doors, because what I may think is a perfect opportunity, could be the completely wrong direction for me to walk in. But those right doors won't start opening until you completely let go and *trust God*. Moment by moment.

I spent a lot of time thinking of an amazing illustration of how God has come through in my life with a miracle. To prove to you that God hears my prayers; because I haven't had to be healed of cancer, nor have I been in a tragic accident and survived, or anything that traumatic. Here's possibly the biggest miracle that's happened to us: *God has loved Randy and me, for the past 36 years, with an amazing, gentle love.* He has dealt gently with both of us and our family. He has graciously guided us away from mistakes, (a lot of them) and softly spoken to us through disappointments. We've taken the gentle nudges and tried to walk closer to God. And God has always been there to teach and love us, through it all. Actually, He's done that for more than fifty years of my life.

That's my big miracle.

Maybe your biggest miracles are the things that God didn't allow to happen to you? Isn't that an amazing thought? Take my advice and stay close to God. He's a gentleman. He won't inhabit your life if you don't invite him in daily. He loves you more than you know, but it's your choice to follow him. Only yours.

Keep working out your *trust muscle*. It is the very starting point of power. Believe that God has a great plan for your life. Have faith that God wants to bless you and your family.

And trust.

Praying together on a different day – with part of our family

Precious Prayer

Over six years ago, my Dad was diagnosed with stage 4 cancer. I was with him and my mom when he got the diagnosis. It was shocking because he was always the picture of health, the life of the party, the man of faith. In less than a month from his first diagnosis, he went to be with Jesus. About a week before he passed, his life-long friend suggested that we should gather all of our family together – my brothers and sisters, the grandkids and great-grandkids – and have a time where my Dad could pray over each of the couples and kids. So, we gathered together, knowing that this could be the last time that Dad would be able to speak into all of our lives like this.

It was amazing.

The couples came and sat in front of Dad, two at a time, as he prayed over our future. He prayed a blessing and laid his hands on each of our heads. He prayed over each of our sons and their wives. They actually videoed all of us and we have a remembrance of the night to look back on and show our grandkids how precious their Papa Moses was. I'll never forget how special it was to have this man of God pray over us.

Maybe this is something you could do this year with your parents or grandparents or even yourself? What a legacy moment.

The value of a praying parent is incredible. The ripple effect will carry on for generations in our family, because of the faith and trust in God that my Dad and Mom lived with. He was brimming with hope. In fact, he always called himself an *'ambassador of Hope'.*

Yeah. That's a cool legacy for Randy and I. We want to be *ambassadors of Hope*. I pray that we are always people who were filled with trust and hope that God is in control. And we know, without a doubt, that nothing is impossible with God. Nothing.

I wish I could say that my prayer-time was a formula for success. I wish it were perfect, but in my limited understanding, I often don't get the answers I want or think I need. However, God's not a short-order cook at Wendy's. He sees far beyond our present circumstances and directs our lives the way he knows is best.

To use our lives for something amazing. And fulfill us.

I know that the deposit of power that is in you will affect more people than you will probably ever really know, this side of heaven.

His power will protect you. His power will motivate you. His power will recharge you, every day, throughout the day, and give you *energy.*

God is the only one who has the big picture of your life. And you can connect to his power.

Take Action:

1) Is it hard for you to trust God completely? If so, why?

_____

_____

_____

2) Do you have a daily prayer time with God? _____

What are some things that are regulars on your prayer list?

_____

_____

_____

3) What are some prayers that you've seen God answer in your own life or someone else's?

_____

_____

_____

4) Do you have a great big miracle(s) prayer that you need God to answer?_____ If so, what?

_____

_____

_____

5) What are some ways you could step out in faith in your own life right now?

_____

_____

_____

6) Choose a verse that inspires you to connect with God for power.

_____

_____

_____

Prayer:

Please say this prayer out loud

Dear Father,

I'm blown away that you, the God of the Universe, love me so much and care about me. You've got the power to change my life, because you're my Creator.

I thank you for my life, my family and my friends. I have so many things to be thankful for. I'm so grateful that you've given me the opportunity to come to you and start fresh every day.

I ask you to help me learn to spend time daily with you – quality time and not rushed. Thank you that there are no limits to what you can do in my life!

I'm excited to become everything you've made me to be. I give all my fears to you daily and I trust that you have every-thing under your control. I know that all things work together for good in my life from this day forward, because I put my trust in you.

I'm ready for your explosive energy.

In Jesus' name,
Amen

Energy Playlist:
Do It Again

Energy Verses

*For God has not given us the spirit of fear, but of **power**...*
II Timothy 1:7 (TPT)

*Everything we could ever need for life and complete devotion to God
has already been deposited in us by his **divine power**.*
II Peter 1:3 (TPT)

*I'm **energized** every time I enter your heavenly sanctuary
to seek more of your **power**.*
Psalm 63:2-4 (TPT)

*And we pray that you would be **energized**
with all his **explosive power**
from the realm of his magnificent glory,
Filling you with great hope*
Colossians 1:11 (TPT)

*God is ready to overwhelm you with **more blessings** than you could
ever imagine so that you'll always be taken care of in every way
and you'll have more than enough to share.
Remember what is written about the one who **trusts in the Lord**...*
II Corinthians 9:8-9 (VOICE)

*For God intended that your faith not be established on man's wisdom
but by **trusting in His almighty power***
I Corinthians 2:5 (TPT)

*And I pray that he would unveil within you the unlimited riches of his glory and favor until supernatural strength floods your innermost being with his divine might and **explosive power**.*
*Then, by constantly using your **faith**,*
the life of Christ will be released deep inside you.
Ephesians 3:16-17 (TPT)

I pray that you will continually experience the immeasurable greatness of
***God's power** made available to you through **faith**.*
*Then your lives will be an advertisement of this **immense power** as it works through you!*
Ephesians 1:19 (TPT)

***Simply join your life with mine**.*
Learn my ways and you'll discover that I'm gentle, humble, easy to please.
You will find refreshment and rest in me.
For all that I require of you will be pleasant and easy to bear.
Matthew 11:29-30 (TPT)

Don't be pulled in different directions or worried about a thing.
***Be saturated in prayer** throughout each day, offering your faith-filled requests before God with **overflowing gratitude**.*
*Tell him every detail of your life, then God's wonderful **peace** that transcends human understanding,*
will make the answers known to you through Jesus Christ.
Philippians 4:6-7 (TPT)

*This is the reason I urge you to **boldly believe** for whatever you ask for in prayer – believe that you have received it and it will be yours.*
Mark 11:24 (TPT)

Energy explodes with power from God

4
Love

For God has not given us the spirit of fear, but of power, love...
II Timothy 1:7 (NKJV)

*Most of all, love each other steadily and unselfishly,
because love makes up for many faults.*
I Peter 4:8 (VOICE)

Let love prevail in your life, words and actions.
I Corinthians 16:14 (MSG)

I'm tired of feeling empty.

I heard a quote recently – *"There are only two core emotions deep inside of all human beings – fear and love. Everything we do is powered by either our fear or our need for love."*

I choose love.

Something was missing

The story of how I met my husband is pretty remarkable. In fact, I've told this story dozens of times over the years to a lot of young girls and guys.

As I told you earlier, I grew up in a sheltered family not understanding the kind of love that existed for me, both as a woman and as a child of God. I was more concerned about how my life looked on the outside, than about the core of Christ's unconditional love that was available to me on the inside.

I left for college at the age of eighteen. It was the first time in my life that I was away from my church, my family and my friends. I had played the violin since I was in junior high school, so I brought my violin with me to college. I was randomly invited to try out for the tv orchestra at my college; surprisingly I made it and I was awarded a full scholarship to the university. Now, I'd love to say that everything went great, but it didn't. Despite this amazing opportunity, I still hadn't discovered the real love of Jesus. My grades suffered. I went on dates, but ended up dissatisfied or bored with guys. I got a little wild, (or the 'good girl' that I thought I was did) drinking at parties for the first time in my life. Over the span of two years, I felt lost. So, at the end of my sophomore year I went home, ready to give up on school and put my future on hold until I could figure out what I really wanted. I cut my hair short. *Ladies, if you are at a low point in your life, stay away from the scissors.* I started eating a lot of chips and cookies and comfort food. I fell back into my old habit of hiding from the world and basically became a hermit. No one on the outside would have understood why I was struggling – I'm sure to them I had no reason to complain. I kept my struggle to myself, because I felt like I had no reason to complain either.

But I was *lost*.

I remember one hot, humid night that summer, running into the cornfield behind my family's home. I was sobbing. I didn't understand why I was feeling this way – I felt alone and confused. Maybe it was some sort of a mini breakdown? All I knew was that something had to change inside of me. *Why am I so lost?* (Remember, this was before I had even met Randy, and of course, before my confrontation with him in Portland; I was already aware that something was wrong.)

I broke. Then, as God, (not luck) would have it, the most incredible thing happened to me a few weeks later.

Randy's parents were pastors, and they would speak at summer youth camps around the country. They had been guest speakers at our church youth camp two years earlier, and I had enjoyed spending time with them during that week. I know this sounds kind of funny, but they were convinced that they could help their son find a wife by bringing back pictures of girls who were in leadership at church camps; I used to help lead songs on the platform at camp, so apparently, I met their criteria. Turns out they were right. In spite of a dozen different pictures of other girls, Randy somehow found my picture in that pile, and felt like God 'told him' that I was the girl *he was going to marry.* I know you're thinking there's no way this happened, but yep, it sure did.

Randy started praying for me while I was at college. For almost two years while I was going through my difficult times, he was praying.

That fall, a few days after I had my God-encounter in the cornfield behind my house, his dad invited my dad to speak at his church in California and invited me to tag along.

Ready for more craziness? A week before the trip, God woke me up in the middle of the night. Tears were streaming down my cheeks, as I pulled out my journal and wrote, *God told me that I'm going to marry Randy Alward.* No kidding. This happened. I even told one of my friends the next day; she gave me a card the day before I flew to California, saying that *"She would be praying for me and God's will for my life".* I still have the journal and the card she gave me.

When I flew into LAX at midnight with my dad, I saw my husband at the gate for the first time. Remember, there wasn't any Facebook or internet yet, so I had never seen a picture of Randy. Thank God, he was handsome and taller than me.

But you know what? I wasn't prepared to meet my Prince Charming. I didn't feel like a princess. I felt fat. I felt homely. My hair was chopped short with a serious mullet.

But this was the most incredible part of this story – Randy saw me for what he knew I could be and would be some day. *I'm not talking about how I looked on the outside,* but the *inside* of me. He saw a vision of the woman God had showed him two years before.

Three days after meeting at the airport, we sat together on the front of his dad's boat, gliding through the dark blue waves of the Pacific Ocean. With the wind in our face and the warm, setting sun on our backs, we turned, and looked at each other and said, *"I have something to tell you. God told me that we're supposed to get married."* We practically said it at the same time.

Later that week, we sat on a cliff overlooking the Pacific Ocean and talked about our future, *(little did we know we would end up raising our kids close to that same beach)*. Ten months later we were married. For over 37 years now.

Randy taught me about one of the most important things in life: unconditional love. He was the first guy who loved me exactly how I was at that moment: *Insecure, mullet and feeling frumpy.* It was, and is the most beautiful thing about my husband. He's not a saint, but boy, does he have the love thing down.

You know what though? Here's what is mind-blowing: Randy is my dream-guy, but I have no guarantee that he'll be here tomorrow. None. The mere fact that he's human, is evidence that he's vulnerable to life and every facet of it.

As well as my husband loved me and still does, God is the only one who can fill the emptiness in my life; that same emptiness that is shared by all humanity

This is the phenomenal truth: *As well as my husband loved me, and still loves me; God is the only one who can fill the emptiness in my life* – that same emptiness that is shared by all humanity. My peace, my joy has to be in the love of God, the love of Jesus Christ.

No one else is capable of filling that void. No one.

Jesus loved me when I couldn't love myself. When I felt frumpy, rejected and lost, Jesus looked at me with open arms and said, *"Cathy, I love you more than you can imagine and I have a plan for your life."* This is unconditional love. Listen to this description of his love:

May your roots go down deep into the soil of God's marvelous **love.**

And may you have the power to understand, as all God's people should, how wide, how long, how high and how deep His love really is.

May you experience the **love of Christ***,*

though it is so great you will never fully understand it.

Ephesians 3:17-19 (TPT)

Our Wedding Day
(My mullet grew out a little)

Love is Kind

Years ago, I went to pick up some donuts for my family and as I walked into the store, I noticed a teenage-girl sitting with her back against the wall and her eyes closed. She looked, for lack of a better term, wasted. I watched her through the window while I waited in line, and something told me that I was supposed to reach out to her.

After I paid for my donuts, I walked outside to the girl and tapped her on her shoulder, *"Hey sweetie, are you okay?"*

She looked up at me and didn't respond. Her long blonde hair was matted, her eyeliner was smeared under her *(pretty, I guessed)* eyes, and she reeked of stale cigarettes.

"Can I give you a ride somewhere?" I asked her.

I was kind of surprised when she got up on her feet and mumbled, *"Yeah, okay".* She told me that her name was Nicole and after having some awkward small talk with her for a few minutes in the car, I think she felt safe with me. She told me that she was in *trouble*, and it sounded like she was being threatened by some very, very unpleasant people.

Oh wow.

I could tell she was scared. The 'momma-bear' in me shifted, from being *concerned* to becoming *alarmed*, and I asked her if she wanted to come over to our house and hang out for a while? She hesitated, but since she clearly didn't have too many other choices, she agreed.

My husband looked shocked when we walked through the door together with the donuts. I introduced Nicole to Randy and I asked her if she'd like to take a shower and borrow a pair of my sweats? While she showered and washed her hair, I washed and dried her clothes and made her a warm breakfast. After her shower and dressed in my comfy sweats, Randy and I sat down with her while she ate. Nicole told us that she had run away from home, but she wouldn't tell us where she was from, even though we prodded her. I'm guessing that she was around 18 or 19 years old. She told us that she'd gotten involved with dealing drugs in our affluent town and that her supplier was giving her a hard time.

She spoke softly; it was hard for her to talk without crying. My heart broke to see the emptiness in her eyes, because she was obviously living with a lot fear.

We offered to help her fly home to her family, wherever that was, but she clearly had no desire to go back to her family. It made me wonder what kind of mess that she had run away from back home? Or who knows? Maybe her family missed her and they were desperately looking for her? Either way, this poor girl was in trouble. We asked her if we could at least pray for her, and she agreed to let us pray.

After we finished, she seemed nervous and she told us that she really needed to get going. She changed back into her freshly-washed clothes and I gave her the rest of the donuts, a few snacks in a bag, and some money; I could tell she didn't know what to say. I drove her to a neighborhood just a few miles from our house and she warned me not to pull up too close to her place, because the creepy dealer might be watching her.

And me, I assumed.

I stopped the car and she got out, but before she shut her car door I called out to her, *"Don't forget that God loves you, Nicole, and he's always there for you, and so am I, if you ever need somebody to talk to."*

She didn't look back.

As I think about that day, one of the things that gives me peace is the hope that this sweet girl recognized the *love of Jesus* in Randy and I - and that she realized that God is real and loves her. So very, very much. I'm sad that I couldn't have done more, but I believe that God used me for this brief moment in time to touch Nicole:

So, chosen by God for this new life of love,
dress in the wardrobe that God picked out for you...compas-
sion, kindness...
*and regardless of what else you put on, **wear love**.*
It's your basic, all-purpose garment.
Never be without it.
Colossians 3:12-14 (TPT)

The most important thing you can do in this life is to just *love,* as often and as big as you can.

That's what the love of Jesus is. Every time you step out of your comfort zone and choose to be kind, you represent the love of Christ.

Because love comes in so many beautiful actions.

Why not pay for the person's groceries in front of you at the grocery store? If someone is removing stuff from their cart because they don't have enough money, that's probably your cue to reach out and help them. There have been times when my husband and I knew that we were supposed to leave a larger tip than normal at a restaurant. Or why not pay for someone's gas or even the person behind you at Starbucks? That was a cool thing to do for a while, remember? Or maybe pay for someone's meal at a restaurant anonymously?

Randy and I were eating at a restaurant while on a road trip and I noticed two very big, kind of scary-looking guys at a booth facing us – they had an intimidating look in their eyes. Maybe they were bouncers at a club? Or come to think of it; maybe they were like that drug dealer who poor Nicole had been so afraid of? Who knows?

I silently watched them as we were eating and I knew we were supposed to do something. As we finished eating our lunch, I told Randy, *"Don't turn around, but I really feel like we should show some love to these guys"*. It was clear that people probably judged them by the way they looked on the outside most of the time, because that's exactly what I had done. What chance did they have to discover the love of Jesus in their everyday lives?

So, we pulled our waitress aside and paid their bill. We walked out without saying anything to them so they didn't feel awkward, but we didn't buy their meal to get a thank you. We did it to show them that someone cared about them, without anything tied to the gift. Simply to show them love. And who knows what the impact of that one simple kindness could have had on the rest of their lives? Maybe, just maybe, they will remember that there really are people who care in the world.

When you show love to someone, it doesn't mean that they have to be weak or little or needy-looking before you help them. There shouldn't be a list of requirements before you reach out and love someone. In fact, the people who have the biggest walls up some-times need the *most love* shown to them. My husband and I have done this very thing many times over the years; I think they used to call it *pay it forward*. Whatever you want to call it, I dare you to shock someone with love.

Love heals relationships

I cut my finger on my blender last night. The edge had been chipped and as I was washing it, it scraped over the index finger on my left hand. I sliced it pretty deeply. My son, who at the time was studying to be a paramedic, (and now he is one) looked at it just to make sure I didn't need stitches. He told me to just make sure to keep it clean. *"Wash it with soap and warm water and use some disinfectant before applying a Band-Aid"*, he said, *"whatever you do, you'll probably have a little scar"*. And I do.

The love of Christ is the disinfectant that we use to clean our hearts and minds on a daily basis. When we're hurt by little or big things on a daily basis, God's love is waiting to heal our pain. That doesn't mean there won't be scars, but it will be a clean wound and most likely avoid infection; or in other words, *bitterness*.

Maybe someone said something hurtful to you. Maybe you're feeling jealous or betrayed. There are so many reasons for us to get hurt or angry. But here's what I do as soon as the hurt happens: *I ask God to fill me with love for the person who offended me.* Does that sound crazy? It's supposed to, because that is *exactly the opposite* of how most human beings respond. Most of my life, I lived way, and I mean way, too sensitively. Sometimes, I felt like the whole world was out to get me. News flash, it's not. Most people are more concerned with what's *happening to them,* then what you may be feeling. They are not, I repeat, they are not out to get you. And if they are, well, you should be the one feeling sorry for them, because it's obvious they need to leave pettiness behind and start enjoying their life. They are the one who is missing out, not you.

You should feel sorry for them.

Here's what I've learned to do during the last several years that has been life-changing for me: If I'm offended by what someone may have said or done to me, I send love to them. I whisper to myself, *"God bless _____, send your love to them."*

I kid you not, it works to take the *stinger* out 99% of the time. And the other 1%, it may just take me an hour or two to say those words and mean it. Even if I don't mean it right away; I still say those words and my feelings will follow. And then I don't dwell on it. I send them love and move on. I know I've done my part, and as long as there isn't anything that I've done to offend them, it's all good.

It's remarkable how quickly doing this dissolves any angry feelings I may be having. Sometimes it takes a while longer before I feel warm and cozy toward them, and sometimes I have to pray this prayer for a few days, or longer. Of course, I'm not perfect. But using the love of Christ is about as close to perfect as you or I will get this side of heaven. That is the power of love.

We get brief opportunities to do the right thing. It's the little love things you do on a daily basis that move you closer to who God created you to be

We get brief opportunities to do the right thing. It's the little love things you do on a daily basis that move you closer to who God created you to be. When you feel yourself hurting from a comment a friend made, *choose love*. When you're angry at your husband for being inconsiderate or selfish, *choose to love*. Choose to let the opportunity teach you how to love in the midst of the hurt.

Read these beautiful verses as a reminder of the kind of love God created us to show to each other:

*If people mistreat or malign you, **bless them**.*
***Always speak blessings**, not curses.*
Romans 12:14 (VOICE)

*Above all, clothe yourselves with **love**,*
which binds us all together in perfect harmony. Colossians 3:14 (TPT)

Be humble. Be gentle. Be patient.
*Tolerate one another in an atmosphere **thick with love.***
Ephesians 4:2 (VOICE)

Let love be the lens you look through

When Randy and I were first married, he shared a very important dream with me: He wanted a boat. His Dad had a boat from the time Randy was a young boy and Randy grew to love everything about boats – family time spent together fishing, water skiing and just enjoying the water. He had tons of fun memories and it was important to him that we started the same kind of memories in our own little family.

In our second year of marriage, Randy was driving home from work and he saw his dream. The heavens parted, angels sang, and behold, the boat he had always wanted was sitting in someone's front yard with a 'For Sale' sign slapped on it. He pulled over and got all the details about this precious gem. It was over twenty-five years old and made of wood, with barely an inch of fiberglass. While it truly could have been used as firewood, Randy saw more. Plus, it had a trailer with two tires that actually worked. He couldn't believe his luck. Because we had always agreed to clear large purchases with each other, he gave me a call. His dream was going to cost us $30 cash, which meant we wouldn't have to sign for a loan. I was so thrilled for him, that I quickly agreed.

He handed over his money, immediately christened his boat 'Vision' – because real fishermen always name their boat and he had a name ready to be used at any moment – and pulled out of the driveway. He was so excited, *(boys, right?)* But now he had to make it home.

My dear, sweet, enthusiastic husband hit a large speed-bump as he was driving down the road with his new boat behind him. *Oops.*

He looked over to the right, out the passenger side window, and saw that *Vision* had jostled off the trailer hitch and was bouncing merrily down the road, *beside his truck*. It would have been hilarious, *(and I really wish we had a video of it)*, but poor Randy was so worried about the boat trailer crashing into another car and causing a major collision, that he slammed his truck into the hull of the boat and pulled to a stop on the side of the road.

Never mind the damage to his truck, his precious new *Vision* was smashed to pieces. Firewood. And before I even had a chance to see it in all of its glory.

When he pulled into our driveway a little later, all that was left was the trailer.

"Where's the boat?" I innocently asked.

He was devastated. He did fix the trailer and sold it for $100, so we thought of it as an investment, but I never got to see *Vision* in all its glory.

Over the years, we've had several different boats. We started small and our boat eventually grew into the one Randy had always envisioned. But on that day years ago, Randy saw his dream through the *lens of love*. He didn't see a pile of kindling that probably wouldn't even float on the water. All he saw was possibility.

Come to think of it, I was once like *Vision* to Randy, too.

That pile of kindling.

Doesn't it often feel like you're looking through a 'blurred lens' at life? The bible tells us that we won't always understand what is happening in our lives, that it will sometimes be confusing, unsettling and stressful, but God wants us to use our *lens of love* to look towards our future.

This involves looking and believing with love. It is the greatest tool we can use. When I first married Randy, he and I weren't perfect. We were poor. We lived in dingy apartments and struggled financially. My personal issues were definitely not worked out. But I promise you from the very start of our marriage, I used the *lens of love* to believe in Randy and our future. I truly believed that our marriage was going to be surrounded by God's favor. Through this *lens of love,* I knew our children would be blessed before we even had them. What gave me this extraordinary vision for our lives? *Love.* I always came back to the deepest, most unconditional love. In spite of numerous mistakes, embarrassments and screwups my husband and I have made, it always came back to the love of Christ. *Always.* And I'm so, so good with that.

Remember the movie *Jerry Maguire?* In the movie, while Jerry is awkwardly eavesdropping in the hall, Dorothy tells her sister why she loves Jerry. *"I love him, I love him for the man he wants to be. And I love him for the man he almost is."* In her silly description of love, she nailed it.

Have you found your vision for your own future? What 'lens' are you looking through for you and your family? Have you been using a *'lens of fear'*? Or a *'lens of doubt'*? Or even a *'lens of pessimism'*? If you are, you're never going to see the miracles that are waiting on the other side of your distorted vision. Your lens is *blurred.*

It all starts with the *'lens of love'.* The *love of God* will direct you and have a profound impact on your life.

No chips, please

I think we're going to be shocked someday, maybe not until heaven, to realize just how important the people we talked to and interacted with every day of our lives were. I'm not just talking about your family. I'm talking about the waitress, the Starbucks barista, the homeless person on the street, the elderly woman struggling in the bathroom, the Target cashier, the young girl on the subway looking lost. Even the single person sitting next to you at church with no friends.

Do you walk around staring at your list of things to get done on your phone and forget, like I often do, to slow down and really let your love shine? I get so busy planning for my future and this book and my husband and our businesses, that I often overlook the second weighty commandment that God gave us:

Love your neighbor as yourself.

Boom.

We all have excuses. *"But they're different than me. They're a different race. They're intimidating. They look weird. They follow a different religion. They have pink or blue or rainbow hair. They are wealthier than me and are probably stuck up. They're better looking than me. They're younger or older than me. They're heavier or skinnier than me. They have a different sexual preference than me. They have different political ideas than I do. They're just different."*

I call that a chip on your shoulder.

My brother-in-law has worked for a well-known fitness company for over 30 years. He's a fitness expert and he's hysterically funny, too. Don't tell him I told you, but we're lucky to have him in our family. Years ago, he made a bet with his oldest son to stop eating any kind of chips for a year. Radical, right? He did it for that year, ended up losing weight and actually didn't miss the chips too much. Guess what? He still doesn't eat chips and he feels great. Not to say he eats perfectly all the time – his wife told us about his midnight ice cream sessions – but he cut something out of his life that was just not necessary.

Just not necessary. Here's a question for you: *Have you been walking around your entire life with a chip on your shoulder towards someone or even an entire group of people?* Maybe you just grew up in a home that had negative experiences with a certain person. Maybe it was joked about or bitterly shared over your family dinners. Maybe it was gossiped about between you and your friends. Maybe you've seen it on the news or in movies or on talk shows. It's amazing how chips can be passed down from generation to generation.

My next critical question is this: *Why do you have to accept these chips as your own when they do not belong to you?* Why the heck do you have to carry someone else's chip, or rather, someone else's *baggage* around every single day? Why, beautiful soul?

The vast – please hear me on this – the *vast* majority of people on this earth are just doing their very best to make it through a day. Even in our spoiled society. Did you hear that? Every single person has their own issues and difficult situations to deal with. In fact, most of the time the grumpy clerk or the rude person standing next to you in line at Walmart has been having either a terrible day, a terrible week or a terrible year. (Just like the *Friend's song*, right?) There's a reason they're acting that way. Or they're just plain shy or awkward around strangers. I used to be. If someone is being rude or they yell at you or make fun of you – I've had all of these things happen to me, multiple times – it's not the end of the world. It's not pleasant, but you're a 'big girl or a big boy' now. It's time to grow up.

Send them love and good vibes in response.

Here's a trick that I use to help me to understand someone: I remember to look at the person and see them as a *little child* – which is truly what all of us are inside. Sure, we might act like we've got it all together and we're super busy and we're impressive and we seem like we don't care; but that's a tactic to protect the *vulnerable child* inside of all of us.

Just look again at the wealthiest people or celebrities in the world. A lot of them are miserable. Or they hide it and we find out later how miserable they really were. Whether they're white, black, brown, yellow or a gorgeous mix, rich or poor, male or female, old or young; people are simply doing their best to figure out this life, make it financially for their family and try to be happy in the middle of it all. Every one of us sometimes feels ignored, treated rudely by different people and isolated. And as a result, I think a lot of us walk around with walls up towards someone, or sometimes an entire group of people. We decide, before even giving someone a chance, that they are against us.

This. Is. A. Lie. You have been duped. No group of people is out to get you. But be aware that the enemy is out to get you. Every single person alive has an enemy who doesn't want them to be happy. The enemy wants to ruin your life and make you walk around with a chip on your shoulder, and carry the weight of *victimhood*. (More about that in Chapter 6.) Victimhood is the wrong hood to live in. It's a miserable and lonely way to live. Victimhood is a tool of the enemy to distract you from enjoying your life today. In fact, we were all created to live in Love, not victimhood: *Love-hood*.

I urge you to learn to let go of the chip on your shoulder. You know what it is, I don't have to tell you. Here's a quick test to see if you have a chip on your shoulder:

* Do you feel like someone thinks they're better than you?
* Do you feel like you're not good enough when you stand by, talk to, walk by, sit next to or even watch someone on social media?
* Do you sometimes feel like it's 'you' against 'them'?
* Have you accepted someone else's offenses as your own?

These are all *chips.*
Listen to this incredible scripture:

*Your ancestors have also been taught "Love your neighbors and hate the one who hates you". However, I say to you, **love your enemy**, bless the one who curses you, do something wonderful for the one who hates you (Whoa), respond to the very ones who persecute you by praying for them. (Boom.)*
For that will reveal your identity as children of your heavenly Father.
Matthew 5:43-45 (TPT)

These past few years have been terribly hard. Our society has become divisive and confusion has filled a lot of us with distrust and hate. So, how do we respond to hate?

We bless our enemy. We do something wonderful for the one who hates us and we pray for the people that persecute us. It seems like the exact opposite of what all those crazy reality shows teach us, but that's kind of Jesus' favorite mode. (Read the verse above again.) Jesus wants us to *'do the exact opposite of what everyone else thinks would be fair.'*

If you can identify with any of the questions above, this is your chance to turn your future around. The enemy would like nothing better than to make you, or even a whole family or community or group of people feel like they're doomed because of the past.

Yet another lie. Be a warrior of love and fight back against the lies with the love of Jesus. The love of Jesus is the only weapon of any worth.

Be kind, for everyone you meet is fighting a hard battle.

Love and Grace

During the horrific Sandy Hook Elementary School shooting, twenty-six students and teachers were gunned down at their school on December 14, 2012, at 9:30 in the morning. It was a senseless tragedy against helpless children and their brave teachers. And it's terrifying to have seen so many other shootings since that day. Through the horror of the weeks following the shooting, I listened to interviews with the parents who had lost these precious, beautiful children with tears running down my cheeks.

One of them said something that made my heart skip a beat.

The parents of Grace, a beautiful little seven-year-old who died in the shooting, said in an interview, *"We don't want to have hate or anger in our hearts. It's okay to be angry. We don't know why this happened. But we can never live with hate. Grace never had an ounce of hate in her."*

I got shivers down my spine when I heard this, and I still do.

To me, this is the definition of the love of Christ.

These parents chose to not let this tragic event turn them into bitter and hateful people. They chose love instead.

They believe there is still good in the world and *beautiful love* waiting ahead for them. If someone who lost a child in this unspeakable way can live their lives with love and let go of hate, I hope I can let go of my own offenses and pain as quickly, and with the same Grace.

Never let evil defeat you, **but defeat evil with good***.*
Romans 12:21 (TPT)

It doesn't get much clearer than that verse.

Maybe you will be the only person in your family who doesn't have a chip on their shoulder. I encourage you to be okay with that, because you are on the *right side of love*. And love wins.

Only love heals and repairs years of hurt.

The generations and your sphere of influence that follow you and live long after you, will have a solid foundation to build their best life, because of your courageous choice. Leave a trail of love behind you everywhere you go. *Let love dominate your life.*

I dare you.

Take Action:

1) What does (unconditional) love mean to you?

_____

_____

_____

2) What are some ways you've seen the love of God in your life?

_____

_____

_____

3) Do you find it hard to love at times? _____ If so, why do you think so?

_____

_____

_____

4) What are some ways you can think of to show love daily to others? What are some creative ways to demonstrate love?

_____

_____

_____

5) Choose a verse that reminds you to be aggressive with love.

_____

_____

_____

Prayer:

Please say this prayer out loud

Father,

*Thank you for loving me. It's amazing that you love me just the way I am, with all my faults and insecurities. I ask you to fill me with your **love** today and every day.*

*Teach me to see the world through the **lens of love,** instead of hate or indifference.*

*Help me to show your **love** daily to everyone I come in contact with – from my spouse, or my boyfriend or girlfriend or my children, to the grocery clerk or my hairdresser, or even a person who may not like me. I want to be an example of the love of Christ.*

*Every time I choose **love** over hate, I help change the world into a more beautiful place. When I grow in your **love,** I feel energy and I will live the most dynamic life possible.*

I pray this in Jesus' name,
Amen

Energy Playlist:
How He Loves

Energy Verses

*For God has not given us the spirit of fear, but of power, **love**...*
2 Timothy 1:7 (TPT)

*Let **love** and kindness be the motivation behind all that you do.*
I Corinthians 16:14 (TPT)

*Most of all, **love** each other steadily and unselfishly,*
*because **love** makes up for many faults.*
I Peter 4:8 (VOICE)

*Let **love** prevail in your life, words and actions.*
I Corinthians 16:14 (MSG)

*For God so **loved** the world that he gave his one and only Son, that*
whoever believes in him shall not perish but have eternal live.
John 3:16 (NIV)

A thief has only one thing in mind – he wants to
steal, slaughter, and destroy.
But I have come to give you everything in abundance,
more than you expect –
life in its fullness until you overflow!
John 10:10 (TPT)

*Speak **blessing**, not cursing, over those who reject and persecute you.*
Celebrate with those who celebrate, and weep with those who grieve.
***Live happily in a spirit of harmony**,*
and be as mindful of another's worth as you are your own...
Never hold a grudge or try to get even,
but plan your life around the noblest
*way to **benefit others**.*
Do your best to live as everybody's friend...
And if your enemy is hungry, buy him lunch!
*Win him over with **kindness**.*
For your surprising generosity will awaken his conscience,
*and God will **reward you with favor**.*
Never let evil defeat you,
*but **defeat evil with good**.*
Romans 12: 14-16a, 17-18, 20-21 (TPT)

*Whoever does not **love** does not know God,*
*because **God is love.***
I John 4:8 (NIV)

Love is the fuel for Energy

5

A Sound Mind

For God has not given us a spirit of fear, but of power,
love and a Sound Mind.
2 Timothy 1:7 (NKJV)

He will continually restore strength to you,
so you will flourish like a well-watered garden...
Isaiah 58:11(TPT)

Every Believer is ultimately responsible for
his or her own conscience
Galatians 6:5 (TPT)

I'm tired of the noise.

When I was a little girl growing up in Ohio, one of my chores was pulling weeds out of the flower beds in front of our home. If we were bored and sitting in front of the TV on a Saturday morning, my parents would kick all of us kids out of the house to pull weeds. Later as a teenager when I got in trouble, I was grounded, and bonus, I was sent outside to pull those pesky weeds.

My Dad tried to plant a vegetable garden out by our old barn one year, and all I remember were the weeds that seemed to strangle the tomatoes and carrots and lettuce, no matter how often we pulled the weeds. Sadly, the garden was not a big success.

Years later, when I was pregnant with my first baby, I was working out in my little yard pulling weeds when my water broke. It was poetic. Digging in the cool dirt, my body seemed to know it was time to birth the seed that had grown inside of me for all those months. Such a beautiful reminder of the cycle of life.

Ironically, I absolutely love anything to do with gardening today because I feel a connection to the earth. So, thanks for that, Mom and Dad – all of the trouble I got into paid off.

This year, Randy and I are planning a brand-new garden on our property. We are sketching, (well, I'm sketching and Randy executes my plans), dreaming, walking, measuring and preparing the soil. It takes a lot of work to plant a garden from nothing. But don't worry, because I have a dream garden in mind that I'm going to shamelessly copy. This garden belongs to none other than our beloved Joanna Gaines of Fixer Upper fame. I'm guessing you've seen the show? My favorite episode is the one where Chip and JoJo start with an empty piece of land, Chip hands JoJo a golden shovel and they start to dig and create this magical garden in their barren backyard. Every detail of this garden is incredible. The carefully planned veggie beds (check!), the planting shed (check!), the fruit trees (check!), the chicken coop and chicken run surrounding the garden so the chickens can eat all the bugs (check and check!) Come on now – they thought of everything. I'm seriously in love. We started our dream garden this spring and I hope JoJo will be proud.

Gardens. Getting rid of the rocks, adding rich compost, lining up the vegetable and flower beds, watering and feeding. Waiting for the circle of life to work its magic. Fragrant. Rich. Fruitful.

Flourish like a well-watered garden

I think of a *sound mind* as our own rich garden that God has gifted each of us with. And we are each ultimately responsible for what we allow to be planted in our thoughts and the peaceful fruit that comes from a sound mind. Because your mind is a powerful place that is capable of changing the trajectory of your life.

In other words, *whoever or whatever controls your mind*, has the power to dictate the outcome of your life.

So how can you have a sound mind? It's not easy. It's still a fight for me every day to protect what I let in my mind, to keep my thoughts on the truth and to feed my mind with power thoughts, God thoughts. I will say I have made some remarkable changes in my thinking over the past few years, but you know, it's not like I was always thinking destructive thoughts or believing a lot of lies...oh wait, it *is* like I was always struggling with my thoughts and believing a lot of lies about myself, about my future, and about the person that God created me to be. Just like every other woman or man alive today, I have been fed a load of crap for years and I had settled in with a bucket of popcorn and accepted a lot of what I heard, watched, or scrolled through from advertisers, marketing, supposed friends, the media, celebrities, religion, social media,

Blah, blah, blah, blah, blah.

Enough.

Wake up. There is a full-out attack on my mind and your mind and it's time to declare war. Think that sounds a little extreme? Think again. You and I have been given the delicate task of guarding what we let into our minds. This may not have been as necessary 100 or even 50 years ago, but times have changed. We no longer have the luxury to sit back passively.

The good news? I promise you that you can change your life when you take control of your mind. It will change your future and, I will be so bold to say, your family's future and legacy.

In the next two chapters, you will look at the revolutionary power of your mind. Too often, we aren't prepared for and don't understand how to handle this powerful gift – your own 'garden' in your mind.

I'm going to show you three ways to:

 ✷ Prepare the soil of your mind
 ✷ Plant the right seeds and water your mind
 ✷ Enjoy the peaceful fruit of a fragrant, healthy garden – a sound mind

Prepare the Soil –

The Toxic noise of technology

May I ask what you've been thinking about lately? That's hard to pin down, isn't it? The noise that surrounds every one of you today is deafening. Your vulnerable mind is being invaded from countless places. The Internet. Social media. The news. Eye-rolling, cringe-worthy reality TV. The list goes on and on. Who would have thought even 50 years ago that you would be living in a virtual storm of visual and audio attacks on your mental well-being? It's no wonder you are stressed out. You can look at your phone at any moment of the day to check on what is happening to thousands of people who you don't even know or probably really should know anything about. Their problems have become your problems. Their victories make you wonder why you can't have what they have.

It says in I Corinthians 14:33 (AMP), *"God is not a God of confusion and disorder but of peace and order"*. Boom! Have we ever had more confusion in the world? Guess what? The toxic noise that surrounds us was not God's idea.

Remember that peaceful place called the Garden of Eden? I'm positive that cool breezes, flickering sunlight through the lush trees, birds singing and quiet communion with God were more God's idea of paradise on earth than our current noisy, confusing world.

I believe without a doubt that the internet and social media is the *Trojan Horse* in our society today. It has slipped into our homes as a gift and in the night, a destructive attack on our minds has been unleashed. Someone said the other day that as your time on the Internet goes up, your sense of well-being, (or peace) goes down. Hmmm, does that sound familiar? Yet through it all, we keep scrolling and listening to random people profess to be the expert and to be the influencer in our life. *That title right there should scare the living daylights out of you.* And you wonder why you are stressed out all the time, why you're left at the end of the day feeling depressed and competing with imaginary enemies?

I'll confess that I let toxic noise into my life far too much: I scroll aimlessly, look up and realize it's been an hour or more. It's probably safe to say you're a victim of toxic noise, too, but who can blame you? Social media is wired to be addictive. And oh boy, is it. This is the secret to Facebook and Instagram's success. Journalist Simon Parker said, *"We compulsively check the site because we never know when the delicious ting of social affirmation may sound"* [7] This is where dopamine comes into the equation. Dopamine is one of the 'feel good' chemicals in our brain. Interacting with the pleasure and reward center of our brain, dopamine – along with other chemicals like serotonin and endorphins – plays a vital role in how happy we feel. Dopamine relates to the reward we receive for any action. In addition to our mood, dopamine also affects movement, memory and focus. Did you get that? Focus. ADHD is common today, but are you surprised? I'm not, because I've struggled with it at times in my life.

The article continues: *"In an unprecedented attack of candor, Sean Parker, one of the founders of Facebook,* (remember Justin Timberlake in the movie, *The Social Network?) recently admitted that the social network was founded not to unite us, but to distract us. The thought process was: How do we consume as much of your time and conscious attention as possible?" Whenever someone likes or comments on a post or photograph",* he said, *"We...give you a little dopamine hit."* These are the 'notifications' that we see pop up in red at the top of the home page. I rarely use Facebook and yet I keep getting notifications for the most random things. Have you noticed this, too? This is the secret to Facebook's success. Over 2.8 billion *(with a B)* people use Facebook. Those hits of dopamine are a gold mine for advertisers.

Our kids have been sucked in, too. Many check their phones dozens of times a day on Instagram or other social platforms, and they're obsessed with the appearance of their feed. I had coffee with several different young women recently and all of them had this in common: They were glued to their phones, nervously preoccupied and their eyes seemed to be glazed over. Honestly, I was tempted to put my hand over their phone and say, "Hey girlfriend, did you hear what I said?

I'd like to say that phone addiction is just a problem with teenagers, but everyone seems to be just as addicted. In fact, social media has tapped into our insecure inner child, a child who craves attention

---

7   Simon Parker, *Has Dopamine got us hooked on Tech?*, theguardian.com, 2018

and digital hugs. Our soft underside bellies of self-doubt, jealousy and competition are exposed almost 24/7 and it's hard to take cover from the attack when we can't or won't put our phones down. And when technology uses you, you become the tool.

The Toxic Noise of Busy

Tick. Tock. Tick. Tock. The metronome of self-imposed busyness. The *beat of busy* just keeps getting faster and faster and faster. Never-ending errands. Endless activities for your kids. Dinners eaten on the go or while staring at your phone. Way too many hours working for money that disappears quicker than you can say Starbucks Venti triple latte with extra foam or house payment or credit card bill. The result of all this busy-ness?

Grumpy children. Sarcastic teenagers. Offended spouses.

I remember back in the 1980's. I worked full time at a bridal store, Randy and I had just had our first baby, we had just helped start a new church and built a new home. Yes, we had a full life, but do you know what I remember? Days were slower and there weren't as many distractions. Our evenings were usually quiet. If we missed a TV show, we missed it. We would take Sunday afternoon drives together. Our family laughed over dinner. We still wrote letters and answered our phones at home with *"Hello, this is the Alward residence".*

And then we started on this crazy digital journey in the early 2000's. I remember the internet being introduced and almost simultaneously, I noticed everyone around me started saying how *'busy they were'.* It was the new catch-phrase: *"I'm sooo busy".* I said it myself all the time. Of course, we had three growing boys and our family had a lot going on, but it made me feel so good to tell my friends and family that I was busy. It made me feel important. Be careful what you pronounce over your life.

Look at this quote from *Andrew Sullivan, "And so, modernity slowly weakened spirituality by design and accident, in favor of commerce; it downplayed silence and mere being in favor of noise and constant action."[8]*

Noise and constant action.

---

8   Andrew Sullivan, *I Used to be a Human Being,* nymag.com, 9/19/2016

Most of us today aren't capable of silence and merely *being* in our lives because we're addicted to busy. Boredom is unfortunately misinterpreted and so we often create unhealthy ways to avoid *merely being*. We long to fill up the silence. And that will sometimes create a problem.

> **Human history is the long terrible story of man**
> **trying to find something other than God**
> **which will make him happy**
> C.S. Lewis

Toxic thoughts

Your mind is a virtual playground for the enemy.

When I was around 18 years old, I was sitting in church on a hot summer night in Ohio, whispering and laughing with my friends, as the visiting speaker finished up the service. He started walking around and praying over a crowd of around 400 people. All of the sudden he walked back towards our row; he pointed to me and asked me to stand.

Me? I was stunned. He began praying over me and I believe, discerned this about me; *"You have the call of God on your life, but you struggle with always thinking that the grass is greener on the other side. You're never satisfied."* I don't remember everything he said, but I remember I cried, and this statement has stuck with me throughout my life, *"You're never satisfied."*

And I *had* always felt like I wasn't good enough or that I needed to change something in my life. I was never satisfied. *That old perfectionism again.* This 'lie' that I need to be perfect has reared its ugly head for a large part of my life. It's the default that my thoughts go to when I let my guard down.

How did my perfectionism impact me? I was extremely self-critical and I had a hard time accepting a mistake or any flaws I had. I would get way too embarrassed when my own ridiculous standards of the way I appeared to others weren't met. Now I realize that a lot of my perfectionism stemmed from fear. Of course, this led to overeating, (because I wouldn't always be the fittest) or if I experienced any sort of set-back or criticism in a relationship, I way over-reacted. I tended to overlook a compliment or even distort other people's opinions about me. I basically took everything way too personally. Can you see how I was sabotaging myself with my own thoughts?

Do you have a default that you have had to fight against in your thinking for years?

I would lay money on it that something immediately came to your mind when I mentioned what *lies* you listen to most of the time.

Maybe you always feel far less than perfect, like me? Or you live with feeling *rejected, ugly,* or *unaccepted,* or you feel *like you'll never get out of debt,* or you *feel fat,* or *not successful,* or *unhappy that you are single,* or *you won't ever get the job* you want, or be *included in a group,* or *forgiven,* or you'll *always be depressed* or any other default thoughts you have about yourself. Each one of us has our own particular lie that we struggle with. Or maybe several. The lies that you have accepted throughout your life are nothing short of lethal.

The lies that you listen to in your mind often have to do with mistakes you've made in your past. I've made plenty, trust me, so I'm well acquainted with this pattern in my mind. The enemy loves to bring up your mistakes when you're making progress toward becoming the person God destined you to become. More often, you bring them up yourself, though. Have you noticed this? When your relationship with your husband starts getting better, a memory of a past mistake poisons the harmony between both of you, hostility simmers and immediately you feel like you're back to square one. *Lie.*

Or you start making great changes in your diet and you are tempted by the See's Candy that was gifted to your family or the homemade chocolate chip cookies that you made for your husband, because he considers cookies part of his love language from you. You have a few cookies and the lie that you hear in your mind is that you're a failure. You will never be able to get in control of your eating. *Lie.*

Or you have struggled with depression throughout your life. You wake up on a Monday morning ready to take on the week with optimism and then a series of little, irritating things happen before it's even noon. The dishwasher breaks, your jeans are too tight, your kids are sick, your husband snaps at you before he leaves the house.

Your emotions take over and you slowly sink into that old familiar sadness and feel defeated. Before noon, you're ready to climb back into bed and pull the covers over your head. *Another lie.*

We have an autopilot that many of us easily slip into: *"I can't do that", "There is no way this will change",* or maybe, *"I'll always be this way".* All of us have a dialog that is running in our head. Speaking of that, did you know that you think over 60,000 thoughts daily and probably close to 90% are exactly the same thoughts as the day before? So, if you've been thinking the same discouraging thoughts for years, they will not, I repeat, your thoughts will not change all by themselves. It's virtually impossible. Like the soil in a garden, your mind is a fertile place and you have to guard what you allow to be planted in your mind.

"Every believer is ultimately responsible for his or her own conscience."
Galatians 6:5 (TPT)

How do I prepare the soil of my mind?

✳ Every morning, don't allow any technology, don't turn on the *Today Show* or any news and *don't look at your phone,* until you've grabbed your cup of coffee and spent time with God alone: Until you've *cleared your soil* and created an atmosphere of quiet in your thoughts. (Look back to Chapter 3 for the reason you connect with God in the morning.)

Be intentional with quiet. Tell the kids this is your sacred time. A good time would be right after breakfast – start a daily habit. *"Mama needs to have her quiet time and guess what? You get to have a quiet time, too!"* If you start the habit early, it will be ingrained in them for life. Can you imagine how powerful that would be for your kids? Maybe now is a good time to teach your kids how to pray or read a good book or watch an inspiring show – not junk – for 45 minutes. Or color a beautiful picture of creation. Or write a sweet note to a friend or their Grandma and Papa. Or maybe do their chores, like pulling weeds.

All of us can find time when we wake up. Maybe you can get to work early and sit in your car to read a devotional or the Bible, pray and just breathe deep for 5 minutes. You'll be surprised how this will help calm you and prepare you for the rest of your day.

God will often whisper to you during these quiet moments of preparing the atmosphere and soil of your mind. At the very least, you begin your day with *rich soil*, a sound mind prepared for whatever may come your way.

✳ Be aware of how often you look at your phone or emails. You need to answer texts and calls, but maybe try to limit the amount of time you scroll on social. Of course, all social media isn't bad; there's a lot of great people on social and it's fun sometimes to find cute clothes or beautiful houses, (I love both), but it's the combination of who you listen to and how often you're listening that can add up to overload. Protect your vulnerable mind.

Be vigilant with the TV shows and news you allow into your home. There are some good shows to watch and there's also depressing and negative stuff on TV. Randy and I started watching a few different series on a cable network and after a few shows, the atmosphere in our house felt so dark and negative that we both decided almost at the same moment to turn off the series. If you feel a cloud of depression in the atmosphere in your home, turn off the negative, wherever the source is coming from. Turn it off and turn on music. Whatever makes you smile, blast it. Or even go outside and go for a walk. Watch your mindset turn around.

✳ Turn off the phone *completely* when it starts to get dark outside, because our bodies need the dark to 'reset' properly. The dark is your built-in cue to 'turn it off'. The blue light from your phone directly affects your body's production of the sleep hormone melatonin. I heard a neurologist say that looking at bright lights or at our phones after dark can even contribute to depression and anxiety. Leave your phone in another room while you sleep. Just leaving my phone in the kitchen to charge at night has allowed me to sleep so much better. Try it, (I'll cover more on sleep in Chapter 7). Read a good book instead. Again, turn some beautiful worship music on in your room or your entire home before your family goes to sleep, and feel it change the atmosphere. You can also connect in a lot of fun ways with your spouse: board games, scrapbooking, all kinds of ways...

✳ You are in charge of how busy your life is. You are. No one else. Even if you're a busy student, or a single mother or a newly married wife, or a married mom with kids at home, or a career woman with kids or an older woman, or on a tight budget or not. Even when we were living in that shabby apartment and we were barely making it month-to-month, I was still in charge of my schedule. And so are you.

You have to understand how to take control of your schedule.

I recommend not putting important things on your calendar until it is okayed by the entire family. I'm not talking about the mundane, everyday errands, etc., I'm talking about your *permanent schedule*. This might sound a little extreme, but the best way to honor your family is to allow each member to have a say in how you spend your time and how each of them spends their time. Ask questions about priorities. Explain your job to your kids to help them understand your time away. Help each other discover what matters the most in the long run. Ask each child what their favorite sport is and stick with that sport. What is your child gifted at? What do they have a deep desire to do? These are all clues to help them eliminate the distractions and decide on one or two priorities, besides their homework, of course. If you spread them too thin, they become mediocre at a lot of things. If you prioritize one or two things, it frees up time to develop skills and eventually valuable habits that will produce incredible fruit in their lives. Don't pick out the extra-curricular activities for your kids on your own; let them have a 51% majority say in the discussion. Same with you. Prioritize what you and your family are gifted at and have a deep desire towards, and you will see some distractions fall away. Your life will free up a little more and you'll find time to breathe and enjoy just *being*.

I understand that circumstances are a lot harder to navigate when you're working around the clock, maybe juggling two jobs or trying to figure out how to just pay your mortgage: again, my husband and I have been there. So, maybe you can't sit down at a regular time every night for dinner, but you can learn to guard your time a *little more carefully*. Be brutal with your schedule.

We all need to guard our time like our family's life is on the line.

Because it is.

Boredom is unfortunately misinterpreted and so, we often create unhealthy ways to avoid merely being

✳ I heard someone say that our 'thoughts are like popups or spam on a poorly filtered internet site'.

Reject, let me repeat, *reject* any thought(s) that does not line up with what God says about you. This could be any thoughts from anyone else but God; even your dear husband, or your family or close friends. If it doesn't line up with the truth, reject it and stop your thinking in its tracks.

This takes practice.

If you've had a near constant stream of criticism for years, it is up to you to reject it. I know what the sting of criticism feels like; I've dealt with it from several important people in my life over the years. When I learned the valuable lesson of stopping the negative noise and verbally saying, *"No, I'm not going to listen to that today"*, that's when I started on another level of peace. Even if I had to tell my own thoughts to stop. This sounds exhausting, but every time, and I mean *every single time,* that I have a thought that is opposite of what I know God created me to be, I stop the thought in its tracks. If it's negative talk from someone, I say to myself, *"No, I'm not accepting that today* and I send love to them. *Send _____ love, God bless them"*, and I move on – so I'm not loading anger or resentment on top of everything else.

You have permission to go ahead and be weird, and talk to yourself: *"No, I'm not going to think bad thoughts about my body right now. No, I refuse to accept that I'm always going to be poor or scraping to make ends meet. No, I do have an amazing future ahead for me. No, I am a loving person and I'm capable of accomplishing everything God wants me to do."*

Stop letting *your thoughts or someone other than God* govern your life. Pull the weeds out and get the soil of your mind properly prepared. Say *NO* and then state a true statement back to the lie in your head. Our brains can be trained to think truth. It's called *neuroplasticity*. Neuroplasticity refers to the lifelong capacity of the brain to change and rewire itself to create new neurons and connections between neurons throughout a lifetime. It simply means your brain has the ability to adapt and change.

Your conscious patterns of thought can be changed

When the enemy has been playing with your mind for your entire life, he knows your patterns of thoughts and your weaknesses. The enemy will try to keep hitting you from every side to keep you defeated. He does not want your mind free from confusion, because he invented confusion. So we need to change our patterns.

Changing a bad pattern to a good pattern reminds me of when I switched around some of the cupboards and drawers in the kitchen the other day. My husband and I were so used to reaching for plates or silverware from one cupboard or drawer, that it took a few weeks to finally get used to looking in the new location for stuff. This is a tiny example of how difficult it can be to retrain your thinking patterns. It's not easy; in fact, it will probably be a daily fight for days, months and sometimes a year or two. But believe me, if I did it, you can, too. Every time I have a perfectionistic or a negative thought, *every time*, I remind myself that I am loved fiercely by the Lord and all of my life is in his hands. I don't have to fret about my performance or my appearance or my future, because it's *his plan* that will produce peace, nothing else.

If you can work on stopping the wrong thoughts, stopping the lies and fiercely guarding your phone time and your schedule, you have prepared your soil – your mind – for planting the right thoughts.

This is when it starts to get good.

Planting the seeds and watering

Find your truth

> The splinter of divided loyalty shatters your compass
> and leaves you **dizzy and confused**.
> James 1:8 (The Voice)

Confusion again.

In this world of spin and scams, people often find it hard to trust anyone. We live in a society that embraces *ethical relativism*. This is the belief that nothing is objectively right or wrong and that the definition of right or wrong depends on the prevailing view of a particular individual, culture or historical period. Sound familiar?

It's creepy that our society has been our Pied Piper for so long.

Our entertainment. Schools. Peers. Media. Celebrities. Politicians. Even religion. We have been deceived far too often and deception is scary, because you're believing something that is often not true, yet it becomes your reality.

But, again, *you alone are in control of your mind.*

Not the media. Not politicians. Not celebrities. Not your peers. No one else.

And when you're not grounded in truth, you're easily duped. This is why you need a safe haven to always come back to when you're attacked from all sides with fake truth. Or ethical relativism.

The first step is to establish clear truth. What does it mean to be a follower of Christ and a person of faith?

True faith in God starts with:

* Acceptance that you are born into sin and need a savior (It's humbling, but it's true)
* Embracing Jesus Christ as your *truth*, your North Star
* Accepting God, his Word and allowing it to work in you
* An inner confidence that trusting in God is enough. Really, He is.

✸ Using your gifts to love God and love on others *generously*

This Christ, this North Star, that we lay our lives down for becomes the *truth* that we will always come back to.

Can I be blunt? Stop listening to every Tom, Dick and Harry as your source:

> *"For what the world says is wisdom*
> *is **actually foolishness in God's eyes**.*
> *As it is written the cleverness of the know-it-alls*
> *becomes the trap that ensnares them.*
> *The Lord sees right through the clever reasonings of the wise*
> *and knows that **it's all a sham**".*
> I Corinthians 3:19-20 (TPT)

> *This is why it is so crucial that we be all the more engaged and attentive to the **truths** that we have heard so that we do not drift off course.*
> Hebrews 2:1 (TPT)

The most important truth I always fall back on, in both the good times and the hardest times in my life, are my favorite 8 words right now: *Trust in the Lord with all your heart.*

Trust.

Trust.

Trust.

I've said it in several of the chapters so far because it is that important. Jesus is your truth and when you face anything, and I mean anything, telling him that you trust him to take care of you will catapult you into a new *peace*, water for the soil of your mind and food for your faith.

So, one of the most important steps you will ever take is to: Stop every thought that is opposed to what God says about you.

Every single thought:

> *Tearing down barriers erected against the truth of God, fitting every*
> (that's every) **loose thought and emotion and impulse** (<u>read that again</u>)
> *into the structure of life shaped by Christ.* (It continues,)
> ***Our tools are ready at hand for clearing the ground***
> (there's your garden, your mind – your mind is like fertile dirt)
> *of every obstruction and building lives of obedience into maturity.*
> II Corinthians 10:5 (MSG)

Guys, it is so much easier to learn to take every single thought captive that doesn't line up with *truth* when your life is humming along pretty smoothly, than to find yourself in a huge fight or financial chaos or sickness or worse; before you have developed the tools to take your thoughts captive and change your thinking.

Marriages have ended because of wrong thoughts. It's true. What might have begun as a wrong thought evolved into a bad attitude, turned into looking for a better attitude somewhere else, which turned into betrayal or rejection or finally, just giving up on your marriage.

Again, training your mind to trust in God takes time. It took me way over a year to learn how to discipline my mind, and I will always be on guard to protect my mind from damaging thoughts. But I promise, *I promise with all my heart,* it gets easier when you master the art of 'taking every thought captive' that opposes trusting God. It does.

I'm going to be blunt again – sorry, this is how I roll – I believe when you won't control your own thoughts, it's called *laziness*. And having a lazy mind is dangerous to your peace. The question is, wouldn't you rather live with peace, no matter what happens to you? 100% I would. I tried living by my emotions for years and I was miserable.

The Peaceful Fruit

After we've prepared the soil of our minds by clearing out the toxic noise, and after we've found our absolute truth of Jesus Christ and planted the seeds of his grace and redemption, that's when we can experience the *fruit* of a life rooted in Him. Our sound minds produce the fruit that has been modeled in Galatians 5:22-23 (TPT), but the fruit, *(the Greek word is actually harvest...hmm?) produced by the Holy Spirit,* (power from Chapter 3) *within you is divine love,* (love from Chapter 4) *in all its varied expressions:*

- ✸ *Joy that overflows* (keep laughing, guys)
- ✸ *Peace that subdues* (Trust subdues our fears)
- ✸ *Patience that endures* (The Greek word is never quitting)
- ✸ *Kindness in action* (The Aramaic word is translated <u>sweetness</u>. Be sweet to yourself, to your husband, to the sales clerk at the grocery store...)

* *A life full of virtue* (visible actions of niceness. i.e. pay for the person behind you at Starbucks or buy a needy family a car – you'll figure it out)
* *Faith that prevails* (trust never stops – even in the middle of a mess – which I've experienced many times throughout my life.)
* *Gentleness of heart* (a soft tone in your voice, affection, humbleness)
* *Strength of spirit* (this is often translated as self-control)

This is the definition of peaceful fruit. The harvest, this fruit mentioned above, is our evidence of a *healthy sound mind*, a healthy garden. A peaceful place we'd all love to live.

My favorite lake with my boys

Glassy Water

Every year since our boys were toddlers, our family has gone to a beautiful lake in Arizona during the summer. Even when we were poor and couldn't afford a boat, we would rent one of the creaky faded blue pontoon boats from the boat dock for the day and chug around the lake, like we were the wealthiest people around.

I can still hear the echoes of the boys giggling as little toddlers in their life jackets and sunscreen-slathered cheeks; and years later, our tanned teenage boys roaring with laughter on the jet ski, wake boarding behind the ski boat, tubing and jumping off of 30-foot cliffs, daring each other to climb higher. The temperature in the air averaged 105 degrees in the summer, so we'd sit in the water for hours talking about life, tossing a football and teasing each other. Laughter, love and peace. In 35 years, I don't think my husband and I have missed a summer going to this special place full of so many memories.

At the end of the day, I'd often put my life jacket on and drive our jet ski out to the middle of the lake. By then, the wind had died down and the water was glass. *Peace* is the only way it could be described; breathtaking mountains surrounded the still water, as the sun set slowly, edged with a rim of pink clouds. I'd turn the jet ski off in the middle of the glass and dip my feet into the cool water.

"Thank you, God," I'd whisper, *"for your peace that surrounds my life."* Those moments sitting by myself out on the jet ski are seared into my memory. I've always said there is something *magical* about the water on this lake.

The water is healing to my soul.

Throughout the year, I'll often visit this peaceful place in my mind when I need to find a retreat from the busyness of my life back at home. I close my eyes and I'm back in the warm sun, sitting on the glassy lake with the pink sky, my toes in the cool water and feeling God all around me.

This is the definition of a sound mind.

Being able to feel that peace any time and in any situation. *Peace that is palpable.* Life slows down and you can breathe deep. *Do you have a peaceful place in your mind to retreat to?* This is where you find God.

When your mind is quiet, when life slows down.

Gardens. Prepare your soil and get rid of the toxic noise. Find the truth of Jesus Christ and plant your healthy seeds. Enjoy the fruit of peace in your sound mind. Your mind was created for peace.

Breathe deep, dear soul, because every moment is another opportunity to dwell in peace.

Take Action:

1) Does your 'auto-pilot' often go negative? _____ What are some thoughts that you battle consistently?

_____

_____

_____

2) Do you think the media and the social network influence you too much? _____

3) How do you find yourself getting caught up with either of these?

_____

_____

_____

4) What are some ways that you can develop a more positive and Godly thought life?

_____

_____

_____

5) What can you subtract from you and your family's life? What can you take out of your life that may be unnecessary and that won't be missed?

_____

_____

_____

6) Choose a verse that reminds you to guard your thoughts and protect your mind.

_____

_____

_____

Prayer:

Please say this prayer out loud

Dear Jesus,

I thank you for my life and I understand that I most likely need a total reformation of how I think. I understand that I am responsible, <u>and no one else</u>, for the thoughts that control my life.

Today I choose to think positive, Godly thoughts. I choose joy over sadness. I choose trust over unbelief. I know that every time I make the choice to reject the negative self-talk, I take another step toward overcoming obstacles, whether real or imagined. I take another step toward my purpose.

*God, **"For you have not given me the spirit of fear, but of power, love and a sound mind"**, II Timothy 1:7 (NKJV).*

You said it, I believe it. I move forward with this promise for my family and me.

*I now have the tools to control my mind and live a fruitful life. This promise is my hope and my **energy**.*

In Jesus' Name,
Amen

Energy Playlist:
Graves to Gardens

Energy Scriptures

For God has not given us a spirit of fear, but of power
*and of love and of a **sound mind.***
II Timothy 1:7 (NKJV)

Then God's wonderful peace that transcends human understanding,
will make the answers known to you through Jesus Christ.
***So keep your thoughts continually fixed on** all that is authentic and*
real, honorable and admirable, beautiful and respectful,
pure and holy, merciful and kind.
*And **fasten your thoughts** on every glorious work of God...*
Philippians 4:7-8 (TPT)

Stop imitating the ideals and opinions of the culture around you,
but be inwardly transformed by the Holy Spirit
through a total reformation of how you think.
This will empower you to discern God's will
as you live a beautiful life,
satisfying and perfect in his eyes.
Romans 12:2 (TPT)

***Perfect, absolute peace** surrounds those*
*whose **imaginations** are consumed with you;*
*they **confidently trust** in you.*
Isaiah 26:3 (TPT)

We destroy arguments and every lofty opinion raised against the
*knowledge of God, and take **every thought** captive to obey Christ...*
II Corinthians 10:3-6 (TPT)

Above all, be careful what you think because your
thoughts control your life.
Proverbs 4:23 (ERV)

*Dear friend guard **Clear Thinking** and
Common Sense with your life;
don't for a minute lose sight of them.
They'll keep your soul alive and well,
they'll keep you fit and attractive.
You'll travel safely, you'll neither tire nor trip. You'll take afternoon
naps without a worry, you'll enjoy a good night's sleep.
No need to panic over alarms or surprises,
or predictions that doomsday's just around the corner,
because God will be right there with you;
he'll keep you **safe and sound**.*
Proverbs 3:21-26 (MSG)

Our Thoughts influence our Energy

6

Overcomer

So, we must let go of every wound that has pierced us,
and the sin we so easily fall into.
Then we will be able to run life's marathon race with
passion and determination,
for the path has been already marked out before us.
Hebrews 12:1 (TPT)

She bends with the wind,
Trials and tribulation may weather her,
Yet, after the storm her beauty blooms,
See her standing there, like steel,
With her roots forever buried,
Deep in her Southern soil.
Nancy B. Brewer

I'm tired of the old story in my head.

Tears fell silently down my cheeks.

It was after midnight and I was in the emergency room at the hospital with my head wrapped in a thick bandage, my teeth were wired shut and I could barely breathe.

Three days earlier, I had undergone double-jaw surgery. That night, my husband had rushed me to the hospital because I was having trouble breathing and the attending physician had suctioned huge blood clots from my nose and put me on a morphine drip to help control my pain. Last year my jaw had bothered me enough for me to finally get evaluated by a surgeon and he had confirmed to me what I had long-suspected; I needed jaw surgery. To help prepare myself – for months before my surgery – I read every blog I could find on the procedure, took the right supplements, exercised and ate healthier; but the actual surgery didn't go as well as I had planned. It turns out that the braces I had years ago weren't the only reason my bite was so bad; I actually had some bones missing in my upper jaw. So, the surgery that my surgeon had told me was going to be five to six-hours, ended up being *eleven-hours long*.

During the months that I recovered, Randy took care of me 24/7 by giving me horrible-tasting medication through a syringe, preparing smoothies in condiment bottles, making me laugh, (well, sort of), massaging my sore neck, rushing me to the ER that scary night and in so many other ways. He was clearly an angel. But even with my angel-husband, the last few months have been, in a word, difficult.

My life came to a grinding halt.

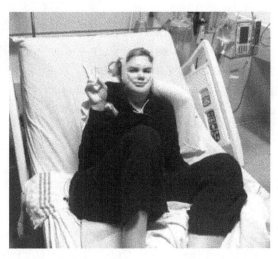

The day after my jaw surgery

I found myself reliant on God to restore me and it propelled me into another level of trust; because God ultimately trumps every plan we might have.

Aren't we cute with our little plans?

Do you know what I've realized as I've gotten older? That God allows trauma to come into your life when he wants you to listen. God allows your world to come to a grinding halt and he says to you in the silence that follows,

"My dear child, it's time to end the harmful patterns that have been controlling your life and be free."

So, whether you've gotten to your trauma yet or not, *(hate to break it to you, but it's kind of inevitable)* this is your opportunity to be healed. This chapter is exactly how I became an overcomer. It took over 50 years for me to really grasp it, because I'm an embarrassingly slow learner, but it is the only way to live exactly the way you were created to live. At first, it's extremely difficult and then, the *magic happens*. It's the simplest thing in the world... and the most wonderful, fulfilling and peaceful way to live.

Are you ready?

Tearing down strongholds

Even though I walked through forgiveness a long time ago, (of course, every day of my life I most likely need God's forgiveness) I had not conquered the *strongholds* that were embedded in me for years: The wrong way of thinking, the wrong place to look for acceptance and the wrong way to establish truth in my very core. I'm not kidding. I had an amazing husband, three healthy sons and a lovely home. I know I was blessed with so much, but I was still leaning on emotional evidence, including my moods, as a measure of my fulfillment. Silly, huh?

Or maybe you know exactly what I'm talking about?

Years ago, Randy had just graduated from college, and we had just moved back to his church in California to be associate pastors, (that's a whole other story). I was still working through my own issues at the time, so it was an adjustment for me. I felt kind of lonely, even though the people at the church were kind. I'll never forget getting a birthday card from a woman in the church. On the front of the card was a little girl hiding in the corner, timid and afraid. I opened the card and the woman had wrote, *"This little girl reminded me of you so much, Happy Birthday!"* Wow. I felt so humiliated. Why on earth would someone point out that I looked like a scared, little insecure girl? But the card made me take a long look at the person I had become. The question I had to ask myself was *"Why am I hiding my true self?"* You already know I was raised in a pastor's home, so you might naturally think that I would have had a special advantage over other people. Not really. In fact, legalism has produced a lot of screwed up adults in the world. When you're raised with an impossible standard of perfectionism, you are left without a safe place to be *genuine*, which in turn creates children who hide their feelings, hide their mistakes and learn to live a lie. If you feel constantly judged and held up to impossible standards, there is not a safe place to *simply be*. Sound familiar? This might be another reason you are not very good at just *being*.

Even though I had gone through childhood forgiveness when we were first married, I hadn't adjusted the dysfunctional patterns I had adapted to as a young woman. I'd often withdraw and become aloof around certain family members and acquaintances if I felt any sort of judgement. I hated criticism and I was overly defensive and I had to 'be right' at all times. My truth had a shaky foundation and I fought the dysfunctional voice in my mind for years. Legalism and fake religious standards did untold damage to my confidence and I hungered for true freedom:

> Come to Me, all who are **weary and heavily burdened**
> *{by **religious rituals** that provide no peace},*
> *and I will give you rest {refreshing your souls with salvation}.*
> Matthew 11:28 (AMP)

Go Deeper

I always believe in solutions instead of band-aids, so we need to go deeper.

Let's start with your mind. As you read in the last chapter, everything starts with a thought. You'd better believe that your thoughts have everything to do with your destiny or God wouldn't have told us to *"Take every thought captive"*. We saw how critical our conscious thoughts were in the last chapter, but in this chapter, we're going to dig deeper into our subconscious.

The subconscious mind is powerful because it controls your system of beliefs and what you think about yourself; for instance, your self-image. It's called mental *homeostatic impulse*. This homeostatic impulse keeps you thinking and repeating the same, often damaging, behavior from your past because it's familiar to you.

Basically, this means you keep repeating damaging behavior for years because you're unaware that your subconscious mind is actually controlling your behavior.

Here's some examples of *homeostatic impulse*: If peace wasn't normal for you, you will learn to resist peace and create conflict. You'll find a partner who treats you the same way an abusive parent did because it feels normal to you. You'll pick fights when it's too peaceful. You'll eat to comfort yourself if food was used as a feel-good drug in your family. Or you'll feel like you're never good enough, because you weren't raised with unconditional love and encouragement. These are just a few of the subconscious thoughts that can control you *without you ever being aware*.

You've been programmed subconsciously to react when *'this'* happens or to stop *'this'* from happening by doing *'this'*. Does that sound familiar to you? The bad news is that your *subconscious* has most likely been controlling your emotions for your entire life.

And that's a scary thought.

If the subconscious mind goes unchecked in a person, it inevitably influences a person's family. And consequently, our unconscious thoughts create a *stronghold*.

I think of a familial stronghold as the bruise of sin that has been in your family for years – ignored, brushed aside and *shushed*. It's the hidden stuff that is rarely dealt with and therefore, sometimes continues on and on for generations; which becomes a stronghold in a family. *Homeostatic impulses* and *strongholds* are close cousins, but a stronghold is more of a conscious deliberate *bad choice* to counter our subconscious toxic thoughts – to fill an emptiness inside, to hide from pain, to cover up fear or sadness or offenses – just to name a few examples.

Here are some specific patterns of strongholds in families: *vicious anger, alcoholism, sexual and physical abuse, gluttony, cheating ways, lying, adultery, uncontrolled spending or perpetual debt, loud and traumatic arguments, neglect, promiscuity, gossiping, unforgiveness, drug abuse, severe and constant criticism, addictive gambling, chronic pessimism, and on and on.* But before you concentrate on the symptoms, let's keep going deeper.

What happened to your mom or dad, (or other authority figure) to cause them to act a certain way? Some say the 'past is just the past' until they see the past repeated in their own lives or even worse, in their children's lives.

Here's a news flash: Most of the time your parents loved you the best way they knew how – not always – but what you saw missing from them as parents was probably missing for them from their parents. *Let that sink in.* The dysfunction you experienced in your family was probably present to some extent in your own parent's childhood.

This may help bring a new dimension of understanding towards your parents. Ancestral trauma and the resulting *strongholds* are often passed down to each generation, and then repeated over and over again through our homeostatic impulses. We unconsciously repeat the stronghold in ourselves and to the next generation.

Unless we stop it.

Speaking of generations, I never really knew any of my grandparents on either side of my family. Both of my grandmas died when I was very young, but I never got to know my grandfathers.

I remember one day, I must have been around 10 years old, when my Dad's father was visiting. I came running through the kitchen and he asked my Dad, *"Is this one of the neighbor kids?"*

"Um, no", I said, *"You're my Grandpa."*

Granted, he had ten kids and lots of grandchildren, *but are you kidding?*

You've been programmed subconsciously to react when 'this' happens or to stop 'this' from happening by doing 'this'. Does that sound familiar to you?

My Mom's dad didn't know us either.

When I was 12 years old, he showed up out of the blue and stayed with our family for a week. He was nice. He watched me swim in our above-ground pool and ate watermelon with us after dinner in the mid-July heat of summer. Two weeks later authorities found him dead in his garage. Grandpa had committed suicide. My brothers and sisters and I sat at his funeral later that week and felt an odd sense of loss, still unaware of the generational influence that had been missing in our family.

Obviously, my Dad and Mom's parents had their own set of issues. In fact, I'm sure that our parents always have a lot more going on from their past than they usually share with their children or anyone for that matter. And always, if whoever raised you; whether a single parent, both parents, divorced parents, adopted or foster parents or any other parenting figure, have approved of and sanctioned *dysfunction* in your family, you have usually *unconsciously* allowed yourself to adapt to life following their example, simply just to fit in and be loved. My parents loved me dearly, but my personal childhood experience was heavily influenced by legalism and the 'guilt-induced theater' that I adapted to, rather handily, around the church. I determined early on to emphasize 'appearances', however damaging it was to my soul.

A tragic misinterpretation of being a functional follower of Christ.

But here's the million-dollar question you need to ask yourself and I had to ask myself; albeit later in life: *Why have we accepted someone else's definition of what is normal without discovering for ourselves how God wants us to live?*

Probably because we grew up trying our best to fit into our family and be accepted and loved and we adapted to the dysfunction the best way we knew how. This is why I call it a *stronghold*, because it has a hold on us that is viciously difficult to be free from. It has, without a doubt, affected our thinking patterns, our emotions and emotional health and sadly, *our very ability to understand the mystery of Christ*. The possibility of peace and the promise of a fulfilled and joyful future.

I'll remind you again, it is not your fault, but you have probably lived in the same tired story for years, simply because your subconscious mind has been conditioned to your past. When the people who raised you don't deal with their pain in a healthy way it does, without question, become your pain. This is a stronghold and it can be detrimental to your well-being.

In this chapter, you will begin to understand why your life has been so hard to navigate at times. And God willing, you will understand why it's *only God* who can *transform* you to become the person He created you to be.

The following are 3 steps to help you:
* ✳ Stop being a victim
* ✳ Discover the secret to truly enjoy your life
* ✳ Be an Overcomer

Step 1 – **Toxic Victimhood**

Be honest with me, a lot of you don't want to be healed, you just want someone to listen to your story. Am I right? You may say, *"Yeah, but you didn't have the abusive father I had. You didn't have a mother that screamed at my dad or me whenever she was upset. You didn't have a spirit of depression that came over your home every day like clock-work. You weren't evaluated by the way you 'performed' on the outside instead of who you were on the inside. You didn't live with a perpetual cloud of guilt over your home. You weren't constantly compared to a sibling as a standard to live up to. You didn't face constant threats of losing your home or even eating your next meal. You weren't raised in a single-parent home.*

You don't understand how horrible it was when my mom or dad couldn't stop drinking. You weren't criticized relentlessly. You didn't face divorce in your family". Maybe I didn't experience all of that; but now that you know part of my own *unique story*, you know that I can relate.

One of the first things I realized in my walk to be free from strongholds, was that I had to let go of calling myself a victim and blaming others for everything wrong in my life. From the time I was a young girl I often felt like everyone was out to get me – I'm not kidding – it was like I had an oozing wound that was never able to heal. So, often if someone said something that made me feel criticized or embarrassed me, I over-reacted and responded with offended feelings. Criticism cut me to my core – like a knife. You might still be thinking, *"But you didn't have it that bad compared to me!"* Maybe I didn't, but it doesn't matter: My issues still culminated in me blaming anyone and everyone else when people didn't say the things I wanted them to say or act how I wanted them to act. If I wasn't in control, I became out of control.

Here's the truth: We talk ourselves into being a victim.

You've probably gotten comfy, *'curled up with your popcorn and your cozy blanket inside your own little victim world'*, blaming everyone else for your circumstances. I know being a victim may feel good for a while but it actually will cause you to suffer more, because you can never, ever get what you want; which is for the trauma or wrongdoing to never have happened. It's an endless cycle.

I can tell you this because I've been there. Yep. And at first it feels so good to feel sorry for yourself, but it quickly disintegrates into a darkness that was obviously designed by the Enemy, and the Enemy would like nothing better than for you to live in that darkness as much as you can. (Remember the darkness in Chapter 2?)

And this darkness will often turn into *depression*. Okay, before you get defensive, I know there are *many* extenuating circumstances that contribute to depression; but when any of us allow ourselves to go down the rabbit hole of comparing our lives to others and feeling sorry for ourselves, it can result in a 'give-up-on-life' heaviness, or classic depression:

*Lift yourself up in pride (**ego**) and you will soon be brought low.*
(or the footnote says, 'to depression').
Proverbs 29:23 (TPT)

Boom! Your ego opens the door to depression. And that is the most surprising truth about the Victim Mentality: *It's almost always your pride or ego working overtime.* You compare your life or situation with others around the clock, you regret bad choices you may have made and feel sorry for yourself; in fact, you feel sorry for yourself most of the time as a victim. And it's clear that always deliberately looking for something to be offended by or mad at somebody, is going to drain you in every area of your life.

It's exhausting.

You might wonder how someone with low self-esteem can have a big ego; but trust me, you can. I still had the old fake religious standards that loomed over my self-worth. I struggled with my uncomfortable jaw and bite and imagined that somehow, I was different from other women because of it. I felt embarrassed a lot as a young woman if I didn't feel like I looked the same as someone else or lived in as nice of a house as another family. Yep. We raised our boys in Southern California by the beach, home of some of the best-looking and wealthiest people in the world, so there was a lot of pressure to fit in and my ego always seemed to show up. And when my ego showed up, I found myself worrying about what others thought about me.

Ego and pride create defensiveness. I was quick to defend myself, without understanding the entire story; because again, I had to be in control. Maybe you understand that feeling of *'always having to be right or to win an argument,'* too? It's a never-ending fight.

Your ego can cause your marriage to fail. You know the drill: *You feel like you need to always be right, you try to change your spouse because you know exactly how they're supposed to act to make 'you happy', you deny your own faults and always point out theirs, you are never satisfied, you thought your life was going to be different than it is in your marriage and you're constantly comparing your life to someone else's marriage or a fake fantasy you have dreamed up.*

My husband and I call them the *'woulda, shoulda', coulda's'* of life.

"I would have done that, I should have done this, or I could have had that." When the fact is, nine times out of ten, if someone took the person who 'wronged' you, (for example, your spouse) out of your life, you'd look for someone else to blame. Again; it's because you are still stuck in the *homeostatic impulses* from your past. This is probably one of the reasons why some people end up getting married over and over again; these are all excuses to serve that same old ego they've had all of their life.

Dr. Daniel Amen, M.D., a psychiatrist and leader in brain health said: *"After 40 years of psychiatric practice with tens of thousands of patients, it has become clear that there's one self-defeating behavior that is guaranteed to ruin your life. What is it? "*

"Blaming others."[9]

Crazy, huh? Blaming someone else for your 'yesterday-life' will always, always ruin your 'tomorrow-life'.

Did you know that the word *offense* actually means *to cause to stumble?* What an incredibly accurate definition of being offended. God designed your path and prepared it specifically for you, but when you blame your emotional well-being today on your past dysfunction, mistakes or offenses of yesterday, you stumble through life.

You stumble when you allow your past issue(s) to become your identity.

As I shared with you earlier in this book, if Joyce Meyer, whose father sexually and physically abused her for eighteen years, can make the decision to forgive him, to stop feeling like a victim and move on – so can you. Joyce even ended up, profoundly, buying her father a beautiful home and taking care of him in his old age. And it wasn't until the end of his life that he accepted Jesus as his Savior. But she loved him extravagantly. And by making this radical and defiant demonstration of love, she vehemently rejected victimhood. She used her tragic past as a 'tool to love and help others', instead of as an 'excuse to stumble around in life'.

---

9   *The #1 Way to Ruin Your Life*, AmenClinics.com, 7/10/20

Blaming someone else for your 'yesterday-life' will always ruin your 'tomorrow-life'

If the parents of Grace, the precious little girl killed by a stranger at her kindergarten one beautiful day, can choose to forgive and to move on, so can you. And If it is still too complicated and difficult for you to find the strength to let go, you will need a professional counselor or mentor to walk you through healing. Only you can decide.

But decide.

It is too great a tragedy to choose to stumble around in victimhood and destroy your God-given right to a bright, redeemed future.

Step 1 is to let go of your ego and stop accepting the <u>victim mentality</u>.

Step 2 – Choose Humble

> *God resists you when you are proud*
> *but multiplies grace and favor when you are* **humble**.
> I Peter 5:5 (TPT)

> *Then when you realize your worthlessness before the Lord,*
> *he will lift you up, encourage and help you.*
> James 4:10 (TPT)

So, you've learned that your *ego* is basically a *huge-ugly-green-slimy-oozing-pus beast*, (this is actually your ego's profile description on Instagram). Remember in the movie *Star Wars*, when Princess Leia had a chain around her neck sitting in front of Jabba the Hut? Google it, if not. Jabba the Hut looks a lot like your ego. *(Swipe left, huh?)*

Maybe print out that picture with the word 'Ego' written by Jabba as a reminder of what your ego represents.

Let me introduce a concept that has transformed me and become one of the most important mindsets in my life: Humility.

Let's be honest: Being humble has a bad reputation. In fact, when you read the word humility, you might have got a bad taste in your mouth. But humility or humbleness is one of the most important character traits that produces blessing and healing for future generations in your family.

Bold statement, right?

If you want to be healed from the inside, it starts with being humble. It doesn't start with self-worth. In fact, you take the authority away from the Enemy in your life when you humble yourself and, *ahem*, submit yourself to God. 'Submitting to God' is another concept that ruffles a lot of feathers.

Ouch.

If you're a woman, you might even argue, *"But what about the 'Me Too Movement'? What about my rights? What about what I deserve?"*

  ✱ *Certainly, it should go without saying that women need to be respected and protected from any kind of abuse, and please know this: If you are facing <u>any</u> <u>kind</u> of abuse, you need to call 911 or contact a church in your area – 99% of churches can direct you to a safe place – that's one of the reasons they are there; you'll be safe. There are people in your community who will help you – please reach out.*

So, of course we've all heard it quoted before, embroidered it on pillows and hopefully understand that, *"God created a woman out of Adam's side because a woman is equal with a man".* Yes, that's true without question.

But humility and submitting to God begins inside of you. In your mind, attitude and soul. And it's a *choice:*

> *Make God the utmost delight and pleasure of your life,*
>   *(the word delight means 'to be **soft and tender'),***
> ***and he will provide for you what you desire the most.***
>   Psalm 37:4 (TPT)

*If you will **humble yourselves** under the mighty hand of God,*
in his good time he will lift you up.
Let him have all your worries and cares,
for he is always thinking about you
And watching everything that concerns you.
I Peter 5:6-7 (TLB)

Yes, the first verse above promises you that if you stay *soft and tender* in your soul before the Lord, he'll provide for you what you desire the most and he will meet every one of your needs. Doesn't that sound amazing?

Are you ready for another truth that may surprise you?

Most people ask themselves, *"What's wrong with me?"* Most people struggle with their confidence – whether they're young, old, black, white, brown or yellow, affluent or needy. Believe it or not, the wealthy girl in California who seems glossy-perfect is just as likely to feel left out and depressed about life as you or I are; I've seen it over and over, and *I know it sounds crazy*, but no one is excluded from this trick. No one. In fact, it's one of the main tactics or tricks of the enemy.

I spent the early part of my life worrying about what others thought of me and protecting that ugly beast of my ego and it was a stupid distraction. Sometimes it felt like I was on a quest to depend on anything but God – *like what others thought about me, whether I got enough 'likes' on social media, whether I was accepted by a group of peers, whether I was thin enough, and an endless list of 'exterior things'* – to make me feel better about myself.

And make no mistake, every time you do ask the question, *"What's wrong with me?"*, the Enemy is ready to help you think of an endless list of things, because he wants you to focus on everything that you think is wrong with you. He doesn't want you to focus on the unique set of abilities and the beautiful soul that God has gifted you with.

Here's the truth that has changed my life: Humility means living every single day *'gratefully imperfect'.*

You are able to say, *"Yep, I'm not perfect, but I'm okay with not being perfect, or my past not being perfect, or my situation I'm dealing* with right now not being perfect". Which translates, "I choose to be happy in the middle of imperfection." I am gratefully imperfect.

That is also the definition of humility.

What else does it mean to be truly humble? Humility is being okay with things not always going your way. It's being okay with the shabby little apartment you live in *right now*. It is being okay with your body *right now*. It's being cool with *getting older* and everything that happens to you as you get older. And I believe that being humble is a safe retreat for your soul.

It is truly the safest place in the world to stay humble before God.

I told you about my double-jaw surgery I went through several months ago – it was dramatic because it needed *to* be dramatic – my bite was out of alignment and it had caused me pain and regret throughout my life, *(hm, sound familiar?)* Like my surgery, God wants you to *allow* him to do dramatic surgery in your life, to remove your ego, and to unlearn the way the world works so you can see how he works. Because God doesn't tend to step into your life until you humble yourself and accept his help: Back to your God-given free will again.

But prepare yourself – because if you allow Jesus to heal your insecurities and that big ugly ego – it will mess up your comfort zone. Big time. I can almost guarantee you that it will be uncomfortable. But do you really need more sugar-coated crap, and Band-Aids, and silly 'likes' on social media, and fake solutions? No. You need to be *healed,* to get your priorities in alignment with God and move on with life; because *without a doubt*:

Only God has the answer to your nagging emptiness. Only God.

I urge you to learn the art of humility, because it is an art. It's painful at times, it took me years to understand its power and I still have to remind myself throughout the day to stay humble; but if you can learn this one secret, you will see God start to turn your life around.

Step 2 is to live in <u>Humility</u>. That's your new 'hood.

Humility is perfect quietness of heart.
It is to expect nothing, to wonder at nothing that is done
to me, to feel nothing done against me. It is to be at
rest when nobody praises me, and when I am blamed or

> ***despised. It is to have a blessed home in the Lord, where
> I can go in and shut the door, and kneel to my Father in
> secret, and am at peace as in a deep sea of calmness, when
> all around and above is trouble.***
> Andrew Murray

Step 3 –**Overcomer**

Our three boys got Randy a record player for Christmas this year. It was a sentimental gift, because every Christmas as a young boy, Randy and his younger sister would sit and listen to a recording of *'A Christmas Carol'* on an old scratchy, well-worn album. In fact, after listening to it every year throughout his childhood, he can still recite it completely, line-by-line, to this day. *("Bah humbug!")* Our oldest son searched for the original recording, but he mistakenly bought the wrong album. When we listened to it together at our family Christmas this year, my husband immediately recognized that it wasn't the same record he had listened to as a little boy. So how did Randy know that it wasn't the same one he'd listened to after all these years?

Because he had memorized every line, every English accent and every scratchy, overly-dramatic musical crescendo.

He just knew.

Beautiful friend, what old, scratchy recording from your past have you been playing over and over in your head for years? Is your mind cluttered with damaging thought-patterns and narratives that you've kept to yourself, but have allowed to be continually played on 'repeat' inside your head? Your unconscious thoughts have kept you thinking and repeating the same, often damaging behavior from your past because it's familiar *to you*; so therefore, you're too cozy, too comfortable living with your fake 'Band-Aids' and fake solutions to change.

You might even be living in survival mode right now – deceiving yourself – because you've chosen to ignore a stronghold in your life. You are using all your energy just to *survive* and that leaves no extra energy for *repair or healing or growth*. That's surely one of the reasons you're tired a lot of the time. But someday, your life will undoubtedly come to a *grinding halt* and a crisis will happen. Or two. And you will be left grasping fake Band-Aids: *like drinking too much or another addictive behavior, out-of-control anger, overspending with credit cards, or 'eating your feelings', chaotic emotions, or letting fear control you, settling into pessimism, or looking to anything else but God to get you through the crisis.*

However; those old solutions will ultimately fail you.

A Grinding Halt

Let me introduce you to my beautiful friend, Tara.

Tara was preparing to get married to the love of her life, Dylan, and their life looked pretty much like every girl's dream: an upcoming fairy tale wedding, a Maui honeymoon, followed by a blissful life together. Tara was dizzy with delight in the months before her wedding, because they were in love. Unfortunately, she was so excited that she ignored the troubling health problems she had been having. She often felt nauseous, she had trouble keeping any food down, and she had been chronically constipated for months. Early on, she did try to get medical help and she went to the ER several times to find out what was wrong, but the doctors never could find out anything wrong with her and they'd send her home, even though she still wasn't feeling well. She lost so much weight that she had to have her wedding dress altered to a smaller size *five times* before her wedding day. She was baffled.

But in spite of all the red flags, Tara and Dylan went ahead with their wedding. They celebrated their marriage with family and friends, and several days after the wedding, they flew to Maui for their honeymoon.

But Tara still felt uneasy. It turned out that she was right to feel uneasy. The very first day at their hotel, Tara got so weak that Dylan had to call for the hotel doctor and the doctor immediately advised him to rush her to the emergency room on the island. At the hospital, the ER doctor ordered a full body scan.

And the news was ominous. Tara found out from that scan that most of her stomach and the surrounding organs were consumed with cancer.

Her world came to a grinding halt.

The doctor told her to get home as quickly as possible and to 'put her affairs in order'. Tara was in shock. She had found out on her *honeymoon* that the possibility of a future with her new husband was at stake. In a matter of days, she had gone from a healthy girl who'd never suffered a single serious illness as a child, to a newlywed with *a one or two percent chance to live*. When she got home, Tara visited some of the top cancer specialists in Southern California.

The last doctor she consulted with advised her, *"Your chances are not good, Tara. It's going to be a long shot for you to live."* This was the first time she had heard it put so bluntly and it felt like a smack in the head to her.

But then the doctor paused and looked at Tara,

"Why can't you be the one in a hundred who beats this cancer?" she asked, *"It can be you."*

"You can be the one who lives."

At that moment, Tara decided to change her belief system. She looked at her husband sitting across from her and she decided to put her *trust in God* and not to rely on a *mindset of fear*. She underwent chemotherapy for ten months, lost her beautiful hair, survived on liquid nutrition from an IV and got down to a mere 82 pounds. She went through radiation therapy and surgery to remove the small nodules that had popped up since her original diagnosis. She had a major hysterectomy, a double mastectomy and reconstructive breast surgery. And unfortunately, in spite of all that, Tara had a recurrence of the cancer three different times. After the second recurrence, she told me that she felt defeated, (which *had* to have been an understatement). She was tired of fighting and utterly exhausted.

Tara was alone one night in her bed at the hospital, and she had a conversation with God. As tears trickled down her face, she whispered, *"I'm having a hard time being positive this time, God."*

It was at this very moment in time when she felt like God spoke to her, *"You are going to be okay. Everything is going to be alright. Just trust in me."*

She said those 9 small words, *"You are going to be okay, just trust me"* changed everything for her. She felt the assurance that she needed to know that God was with her through *every step of her life*.

She decided to be a warrior, with her faith stronger than ever.

And today Tara is cancer-free.

This sweet girl had a one or two percent chance of surviving, but she chose to live in a dramatically new belief system of trust in God alone. Not to dwell in her old fear or to use *emotional Band-Aids* to limp through her crisis. She trusted Jesus Christ to redeem her future. She chose to walk on the path that God has prepared for her. Definitely not her original path-choice, but an infinitely better path – because she is confident that God is directing her steps.

And that's the best place to be in the whole world.

She *trusted*, even though she wasn't exactly sure what God's plan was. But she trusted God – *because the truth and power of trusting God overcomes any old narrative we may have in our head.*

I so wish you could meet Tara, because her joy is contagious.

She is an *overcomer*, not a victim, because she's confident and trusting that God is directing her steps.

> *The weapons of the war we're fighting are **not of this world***
> *but are powered by God and*
> *effective at tearing down the*
> **strongholds erected against His truth.**
> *We are demolishing arguments and ideas,*
> *every high-and-mighty philosophy*
> *that pits itself against the knowledge of the one true God.*
> II Corinthians 10:4-5 (MSG)

Power in the Name of Jesus

What is the stronghold in your life that is erected against *God's truth*? Listen again to this incredible verse:

> **Trust in the Lord completely,**
> *and do not rely on your own opinions.*
> *With all your heart rely on him to guide you,*
> And **he will lead you in every decision you make.**
> Proverbs 3:5 (TPT)

What are 'your own opinions'? Your own opinions are the scratchy, well-worn record that's on repeat in your head. And I know, *believe me,* I know there's a comfort in old patterns.

In fact, I guarantee you that the more *deeply-rooted* your old way of thinking is inside your head, whether from an intimidating family situation, or simply that you have unknowingly accepted a stronghold to help you cope with life; the longer it will take to change your narrative. But those old patterns are holding you back from the better path that God has waiting for you. Your old tricks to fill the emptiness that everyone of us has inside of us, will fail you; eventually. Strongholds are cheap and, often dangerous, excuses to fill an emptiness that genuinely can only be filled by Jesus.

So, how do you get rid of the old recording in your head?

You *speak to your thoughts* instead of just *listening to your thoughts*. In fact, you can no longer live with a passive mindset – you simply can't be lazy about what you believe anymore. We have to be able to distinguish between human FEELINGS and human NARRATIVES that control us in our heads. Of course, it's okay to have emotions, but it's when our feelings are controlled by the narrative in our head, that's when it's dangerous. This is the 'hard part' I wrote about early in this chapter. Just like I said that it's hard to change your thoughts in Chapter 5, it's even harder to change your belief system, your *homeostatic impulses* and to tear down the strongholds from years long past. Why? Because of that *old, stinking ego*. Again. Remember old Jabba? Your *ego* is always going to try to talk you out of any changes you try to make.

But change is possible, no matter how old you are. I'm an 'empty-nester-grandma-married-thirty-seven-years' woman, and after I became aware of my thought patterns, I slowly changed the unconscious thoughts in my head.

Every time that old scratchy recording starts up, I aggressively stop it.

My *'old way of thinking'* actually reminds me of that ugly mullet I used to have; remember the alluring and attractive haircut I had way back when I first met my husband at the airport that night?

It was just wrong.

Your *'old way of thinking'* can be compared to this: Everyone in your family decided – without a consensus vote – that the entire family should keep on 'rocking' *mullets* forever. But friend, even if *everyone else* in your family decided it's a great idea, *doesn't mean that it's a great idea.*

It is most definitely not. *(Sorry, Billy Ray.)*

And, believe me, even though everyone else in your family chooses to think, respond or act a certain way, doesn't mean that *you* have to.

You have the choice. It's up to *you* to stop the old thoughts that contradict truth.

And humble yourself.

And trust Jesus.

At first it was tough, but I've slowly re-programmed my thought patterns. It didn't happen overnight. Honestly, it probably took me a few years to *rely on my trust in Jesus*, every time, and to stop listening to the old recording, the old narrative in my head.

But I found another powerful weapon to help me *overcome*:

*For we have the living Word of God, which is full of **energy**,*
and it pierces more sharply than a two-edged sword.
It will even penetrate to the very core of our being
where soul and spirit, bone and marrow meet!
It interprets and reveals
the true thoughts and secret motives
of our hearts.
Hebrews 4:12 (TPT)

What a cool verse. The Word of God is full of *energy* (yes!) and it's capable of revealing to us our hidden, subconscious thoughts. Basically, scripture helps us discern if the old narrative in our heads is 'messed up'. It was crucial for me to use scripture to combat my old thoughts. Scripture helped reveal the narrative that had been playing over and over in my head, since I was a girl and a young woman. *I used It – and use it – as an offensive attack against my strongholds.*

Here's a few scriptural responses that I used against wrong thought-patterns and strongholds:

* ✶ Fear of people – RESPONSE: *Fear of man is a dangerous trap, but to trust in God means safety.* Proverbs 29:25 (TLB)

* Uncontrolled anger- RESPONSE: *Whoever is patient and slow to anger shows great understanding, but whoever has a quick temper magnifies his foolishness.* Proverbs 14:29 (VOICE)
* Being offended easily – RESPONSE: *When you are insulted, be quick to forgive and forget it, for you are virtuous when you overlook an offense.* Proverbs 19:11 (TPT)
* Respecting fake religion more than Jesus Christ -RESPONSE: *Are you tired? Worn out? Burned out on religion? Come to me. Get away with me and you'll recover your life.* Matthew 11:28 (MSG)
* Judging others because their sin is different than mine – RESPONSE: *You hypocrite (play-actor, pretender), first get the log out of your own eye, and then you will see clearly to take the speck out of your brother's eye.* Matthew 7:5 (AMP)

I now aggressively stop my wrong thinking and I use scripture to respond to each stronghold in my life. As often as I remember or need to do it. Only you can name the stronghold you've been using as a Band-Aid to cover up that old narrative inside your head. Don't overthink it: it will be obvious.

Whatever has continuously stolen your peace over the years is, without a doubt, your *stronghold.* The good news is now that you can identify it, it's already begun to lose its power.

Here's a simple hack – I simply Google whatever I have struggled with, maybe for years: like 'verses about criticism', print the scripture and hang it on my bathroom mirror, or in my car or on my desk. Or I write it in my prayer journal. But the best practice is to memorize it. It's crazy how scriptures will pop up in my head late at night or while I'm showering or driving in the car.

The strongholds that have controlled me have lost their power. But just like I still have numbness from my jaw surgery, it's taken time for me to be healed from the numbness or narrative I had been living with, obliviously, for years. But my jaw is getting a tiny bit better day-by-day. Slowly. Just like changing the narrative in my head. Overcoming takes time. But that's okay.

I'm not perfect, but because of Jesus Christ, *I am an overcomer.*
Stop dwelling on the past.

Don't even remember these former things.
I am doing something brand new, something unheard of.
Even now it sprouts and grows and matures.
Don't you perceive it?
Isaiah 43:18-19a (TPT)

Don't you perceive it? God is doing something brand new in you. Just like Tara knew without a doubt that God was in control and she was going to be *okay* no matter what happened to her, you can now choose to trust that your life is going to be okay. Your belief system is established and founded on Jesus Christ.

Beautiful one, this is your opportunity to end the harmful patterns that may have been controlling your life and be free. The decision to break free from the old narrative in your head will affect your *family* for generations. You may not even understand the influence of your decision until Heaven. But, like dropping a pebble in a beautiful cool lake, the ripples of your decision will continue, on and on.

It can begin with you, because no one has ever cared for you like Jesus.

Take Action:

1) Have you found yourself always blaming someone else for your life today?_____ Be honest, in what way do you sometimes feel like a victim?

   _____

   _____

   _____

2) Do you struggle with the woulda', shoulda', coulda's of life? In what way?

   _____

   _____

   _____

3) In what way(s) has your ego been holding you back or causing you to stumble? What are some masks that you wear? (i.e. "I'm not pretty enough, I'm too fat to feel happy, I've made too many mistakes to deserve God's best"...)

   _____

   _____

   _____

4) Can you identify an alarming pattern of behavior(s) in your family that doesn't line up with God's truth?

   _____

   _____

   _____

5) If you really take a moment to' think about what you think about', what are some of the unconscious, damaging thoughts that you now realize you've been allowing yourself to be

controlled by? (i.e. "I never felt good enough because of 'fake standards' from religion, a parent defining for you what you're supposed to look like or act like or do"...)

_____

_____

_____

6) What are some new, powerful narratives that you can now use to change the damaging, unconscious thoughts that have been controlling you, possibly for years?
(Example: 'I repeated over and over to myself Proverbs 3:5-6. It became my default way of thinking after a year or two. It will take time to change your subconscious narrative. Please be patient. Don't get discouraged – it will be worth it, I promise.)

_____

_____

_____

7) Choose a verse that inspires you to take control of the story in your head.

_____

_____

_____

Prayer:

Please say this prayer out loud

Dear Jesus,

*I understand that the family I was raised in can often control the narrative over my life and inside my head. I ask you to heal me from any wrong beliefs I may have about myself. I want my life to line up with what **you say** about me, not what anyone else says.*

***I don't want to waste my life being a victim.** It's a waste of my time here on this earth, because my life will go so fast. Don't let me waste my life.*

***I choose to be humble.** It doesn't put me at a disadvantage; it puts me in your hands and opens up my life to blessing.*

*In the Name of Jesus, I reject any curses or lies that have been a part of my family and I ask you to **heal the strongholds** that may have been in my family for generations.*

*I am responsible, and I make the choice to stop listening to the lies of the enemy and to walk in freedom. I thank you that in your presence, **I Am Free**.*

In the mighty Name of Jesus,

Amen

(Please say this prayer as often as you need to, to overcome the spiritual strongholds you may have faced for a long time in your life: When the enemy tries to lie to you and tell you that you'll never change; read this prayer again and tell the enemy,
"Jesus Christ has made me an Overcomer and I'm never going back."
Be free.)

Energy Playlist:
No One Ever Cared for Me like Jesus

Energy Scriptures

Humble yourselves, therefore, under the mighty hand of God,
so at the proper time he may exalt you.
I Peter 5:6 (ESV)

*I've kept my integrity by **surrendering to him**.*
*And so the Lord has rewarded me with his **blessing**.*
Psalm 18:24 (TPT)

*Let me be clear, the Anointed One has set us **free** –*
*not partially, but **completely and wonderfully free**!*
*We must always cherish this **truth** and*
stubbornly refuse to go back into the bondage of our past.
Galatians 5:1 (TPT)

Are you weary, carrying a heavy burden? Then come to me.
I will refresh your life, for I am your oasis.
Simply join your life with mine. Learn my ways and
you'll discover that I'm gentle, humble, easy to please.
You will find refreshment and rest in me.
*For **all that I require of you will be pleasant and easy to bear**.*
Matthew 11:28-30 (TPT)

A thief has only one thing in mind – he wants to steal, slaughter, and
destroy. But I have come to give you
everything in abundance, more than you expect –
***life in its fullness until you overflow**!*
John 10:10 (TPT)

So, we must let go of every wound that has pierced us,
and the sin we so easily fall into.
Then we will be able to run life's marathon race with
passion and determination,
for the path has been already marked out before us.
Hebrews 12:1 (TPT)

Even though you intended to harm me,
*God intended it **only for good**,*
*and **through me**,*
*He preserved the **lives of countless people**,*
as He is still doing today.
Genesis 50:19-20 (VOICE)

The person who loves his life and pampers himself will miss true life!
But the one who detaches his life from this world
and abandons himself to me,
*will **find true life and enjoy it forever!***
John 12:25 (TPT)

And then, after your brief suffering, the God of all loving grace,
who has called you to share in his eternal glory in Christ,
*will personally and **powerfully restore you and***
make you stronger than ever.
Yes, he will set you firmly in place and build you up.
I Peter 5:10 (TPT)

So think of it this way:
*if the Son comes to make you **free**,*
you will really be free.
John 8:36 (VOICE)

Be free and filled with God's Energy

7

Your Atmosphere

Strength and dignity are her clothing and
her position is strong and secure;
And she smiles at the future
(knowing that she and her family are prepared).
Proverbs 31:25 (AMP)

But who do you think you are to second-guess God?
How could a human being molded out of clay
say to the one who molded him,
"Why in the world did you make me this way?"
Romans 9:20 (TPT)

I'm tired of a messy atmosphere.

We have a 110-pound golden lab named Hooper and our family absolutely adores him. We picked him out of the litter as a puppy precisely because we thought he was docile and calm, but he ended up being quite the opposite; he's full of energy, strong-willed and when I take him on walks around our neighborhood, he usually ends up taking *me* for a walk.

One day, I was walking Hooper – or rather, he was walking me

– and we passed a lady on the sidewalk with two little dogs. As usual, Hooper tried to show some love to the dogs, but the dogs wanted nothing to do with him and started fighting back. I got tangled in the middle of the scuffle, and as I struggled to drag Hooper away from the dogs by his leash, I spun around and ran smack into a cement streetlight. Hard. *What were the odds?* I knew I was hurt. I found out later that I had a separated shoulder and would have to have my arm in a sling for about 2 months.

Well, my injury seemed like a perfect excuse for me to stop exercising and to overindulge on junk food and snacks, while I watched marathon chick flicks on the couch. Because of that, I ended up gaining about 15 or so pounds; not including the 15 extra pounds I had already been carrying. After my shoulder was feeling better a few months later, I went to a spa in California to celebrate a friend's 50th birthday with a few other girls. When I saw the pictures that my friends had taken that weekend, I was mortified to see the weight I had gained. *(Sometimes it takes a picture, right?)* I didn't mention it to anyone, but I knew something had to change. Besides feeling puffy, I had no *energy;* I was always tired and slightly depressed.

This was my wake-up call.

I walked into my gym a few days later, and even though I felt awkward, I asked to talk to a trainer. To my dismay, the man who helped me immediately took my body fat measurement and my weight, (you don't want to know). We decided together on a healthy goal weight and then figured out the number of sessions that it would take for me to reach my goal. I left dazed and a little concerned with how I was going to pay for it because I hadn't even talked to my husband. But I had a plan. I went through my old, never-used gold jewelry when I got home and used the money I made from the sale to help pay for my session package. It was genius! Making a financial commitment helped me get started on making a big change in my life. I sent out an email to some of my closest friends and told them I had signed up with a trainer and I was starting a new program to get healthy. Even though a few friends said it wasn't necessary and I looked fine, they were all supportive. The first training sessions were embarrassing and challenging, but I pushed through them. Slowly, I started longer cardio sessions on my own and learned it was okay to sweat. It was okay to get out of breath. I scheduled regular workouts and didn't allow myself to feel guilty about spending money and time on my health.

I talked to my trainer about diet and 'what was healthy', and my eating habits slowly changed. He strongly advised me *not* to go on a diet and gave me some ideas for nutritious eating instead of dieting. I asked a lot of questions and learned how to make smarter choices to promote *energy* every day of my life. I went through moments of failure, but slowly, I started to feel more *energetic* and just plain happier. I started losing about two pounds a week, and in a few months, I had reached a healthier weight. My whole mindset began to change about food and taking care of myself.

Gratefully Imperfect

Health isn't a one-size-fits-all and may not look the same for everyone. What may be a healthy weight for you could be completely different for someone else.

My two sisters and I look completely different. My oldest sister, Debbie is nearly deaf and has worn hearing aids for years. Then about ten years ago, she came close to death with a sudden illness, consequently lost a lot of her vision and today it's hard for her to both see or hear. But she is *beautiful*. She appreciates every moment, usually with a keen sense of humor, *(I tell myself we have that in common)* even though she struggles with enormous health challenges. The cards that she's been dealt in her life don't seem fair, but she makes the choice every day to appreciate and enjoy her life.

My other sister, Becky, was diagnosed with Multiple Sclerosis and survived cancer earlier in her life. Even though MS notoriously drains you of energy, I am constantly amazed at the energy she has. She is beautiful and full of life and humor. She is one of the girls in my life who I can laugh so hard with, that I can 'barely breathe'. I've seen both of my sisters go through tremendous health challenges and come out shining. They are my heroes of strength and beauty. My sisters and I are completely different, but each of us is unique and *gratefully imperfect*.

We are all unique. It's a fact and a cool and wonderfully imperfect part of God's creation. You are different. I am different.

I've also arrived at the age that my hormones are pretty crazy and it's not easy to stay in shape. I get bloated easily, and my weight goes up and down on the scale. I'm as gratefully imperfect as you are, sis. We're in this together. Whether you have your mother's thighs, (I kind of do) or your father's nose, (I kind of do), there will never, ever be another you or me. We can choose to be *gratefully imperfect* and appreciate our strong thighs and curvy waist. Or our muffin top. Or our flabby arms. Or our thinning hair. Or the lines on our forehead and our beautiful crow's feet. Even our advancing cellulite. We all have a list of perceived imperfections.

Helen Keller, who was blind and deaf, was quoted as saying, *"Instead of comparing our lot with that of those who are more fortunate than we are, we should compare it with the lot of the majority of our fellow men. It then appears that we are among the privileged."* And wouldn't you agree with me that she had a few things to complain about? That's why I'm not going to sit around and complain about everything 'I perceive' to be wrong with me. Of course, I'm not perfect, and neither are you. But, when you constantly talk about what you 'perceive' to be an imperfection about yourself, the mind and body experience these recollections as though they are actually occurring. A study found that *"even just a half hour of complaining every day can physically damage your brain"*.[10] And that leads to low energy and negative repetitive behavior that sabotages your health.

Like if you always say, *"I look so fat"* or *"I just can't stop eating potato chips or ice cream"*, it becomes a self-fulfilling prophecy. Your body says back to you, *"Ok, boss, I'll help make you fat, or "Ok, you need to have more ice cream"*. I've seen it with women: the girls who keep complaining about their lack of self-control with chocolate or their chubby stomach or thick thighs, always seem to struggle with that very area that they focus on. Every time, like clockwork. So, it starts with controlling your thoughts and what you say to yourself and to others about your body. In fact, my own positive self-talk is the most important motivation I need to be a healthy, energetic woman.

---

10   Stanford News Service, *news.stanford.edu; 8/14/96*

Of course, I'm not always perfect, but I deliberately try to use positive self-talk. But not always.

Excuses, excuses

When I moved up to Oregon from perpetually sunny California a few years ago, I used several excuses to explain some weight gain and the low *energy* I felt as a result: "I'm an empty nester, living on the 22nd floor in a high-rise, it rains too much here and I need comfort food." One night we were out to dinner with my son and his wife, and I made the mistake of saying something like, *"I've put on weight because of your Dad - he loves his comfort food and it's hard for me not to eat all the yummy stuff with him".*

My son called me out. *"You can't blame Dad for what you eat,"* he teased me, *"You're responsible for yourself."* He laughed, but *ouch.* That was so true. I had to stop making convenient excuses.

I'm learning to be grateful for every phase of my life, including way back when I struggled to lose weight after gaining 50 pounds for each of my babies, and now that I've set new goals to see my muscles again. So, whether you're a freshman in college and you've gained the *freshman 15,* (did that), *or you're a young mother who can find no time to exercise,* (did that, too), *or maybe you're a mature woman who is struggling with hormonal changes,* (doing that now), I believe God wants us to live our life with an attitude of excellence:

An excellent woman
{one who is spiritual, capable, intelligent, and virtuous},
Who can find her?
Her value is more precious than jewels
And her worth is far above rubies or pearls.
Proverbs 31:10 (AMP)

Excellence does not depend on having more money or being prettier than someone or being thinner than someone or having more stuff than someone. Excellence is being responsible for the *atmosphere* in your home and, consequently, your body. Because the atmosphere you live in will affect the way you treat your body; I believe they go hand-in-hand.

Therefore, *'excellence is a mindset empowered and elevated within an organized atmosphere'*: both your *home and body*.

I've talked a lot about spiritual and mental 'clutter' in earlier chapters, but physical clutter can, and will be, equally damaging. It doesn't matter if you're rich, poor or somewhere in between, a large percentage of people are inundated with clutter. I'll confess, even though I'm a self-proclaimed 'organizer-boss', I'm guilty of collecting more 'stuff', without stepping back and taking inventory of what my family might genuinely need.

A lot of what we have stored - in cupboards or in the attic or out in the garage or in Rubbermaid boxes in expensive storage units - is pretty much useless. It just ends up taking up space and, at the end of the day, drains our *energy*. If you are ready to make a change in your atmosphere, this is your chance to *start fresh*. Just like you wouldn't move into a new home without a deep, sanitizing cleaning, you really can't change up your body and home without first getting rid of the chaotic clutter. Baby steps, guys.

Here we go…

Excellence is a mindset empowered and elevated within an organized atmosphere: in both your home and body

Your Atmosphere - Your Home

You can't overestimate the importance of living in an organized and clean environment - it's critical to your *energy*. I've designed and staged 'homes-to-flip' for years, and I've worked for a few realtors who hired me to walk through a house going on the market and create a checklist for the owners; to help them reduce clutter and stage their home. I witnessed first-hand, homes both in total chaos and homes at the opposite end of the spectrum; clean and functional environments. The difference in the *atmosphere* of both of these types of homes was palpable.

I felt it.

So, let's start with the *atmosphere* of your own home. I'm going to hit each step as quickly as possible, but each step is a move in the right direction. I suggest taking one day to tackle each room.

Remember, changing the atmosphere in your home starts with tackling what is right in front of you. Start with small steps.

* **Bedroom:** Make your bed every day. I'm definitely not a perfect house keeper, but I've made my bed every day since I was married, (except if one of us was sick or we left in a hurry because we were running late; but even when I'm late, I still try to make my bed). When your bed is made, it signals your brain that your day has *started* and actually gives you energy to get going. Wash your sheets once a week; in fact, buy two sets of sheets to rotate. Keep your bedside tables and the inside drawers organized, and the space underneath your bed completely clutter free. Your bedroom should only have a few pieces of furniture with minimal clutter. Every bit of extra clutter in your bedroom registers as stress on your brain; yes, I'm talking about the kids' toys, the office desk, the dusty elliptical and the piles of laundry. I suggest installing dimmers on any overhead lighting and possibly room darkening drapes to improve your sleep: It's been proven that you sleep better in a dark, cool room. As I mentioned earlier, leave all your electronic devices plugged in at another location in the house a few hours before sleep. Even the light from a digital clock can interrupt your sleep. Remember, before there was electricity, people slept in pitch black rooms.

    (*Magic!* You're sleeping in an exclusive Spa Hotel.)

* **Bathroom:** In your bathroom, remove all the items from every drawer, cupboard and the shower and set everything down on a large towel on the floor. With a trash can next to you, go through each and every item, and throw away anything you haven't used in 3 months. Pitch it or give it away. Wipe off

everything with a damp cloth and use new baskets or plastic bins to categorize makeup, creams, etc. Clean all your make-up brushes every week. I use baggies to sort stuff and store in baskets with labels. Experiment and find the best creams, shampoos, conditioners, etc. Then, stick with them. It's so much better than having ten bottles of 'something'. Deep-clean the floors, toilet and shower and clean them regularly. Replace old ratty shower curtains and rugs with new. Buy new white, fluffy towels. Leave a small vase with fresh flowers by your sink, a fragrant candle and maybe small potted plants in both your bath and bedroom - it improves the air quality. Also, purchase a tall mirror to take a final look at your entire outfit before you leave for the day.

* **Closet:** Remove everything from your closet. Make a pile to keep, a pile to give away and a trash pile. You know the drill. Here's an idea: Decide on the best colors for your skin and stick with those colors for most of your clothes. I don't look good in bright colors, period, so my closet looks very autumn-y; but it makes me happy and it works for me. I also group all my hanging tops and dresses by colors - this is from working at the mall back in the day - white to black. Go through your shoes and only keep the most comfortable, clean and classy ones. Same goes for purses, jewelry and accessories: try to keep the items that are timeless and in good condition. Sell or give everything else away.

* **Kitchen:** Pull everything out of the cupboards and drawers in your kitchen and only keep what you *use*; give away every-thing else or, if it's junk, throw it away. Be ruthless. Purchase new storage bins and labels. Wipe down the interiors and organize the food in the pantry by categories. You can buy beautiful dishes inexpensively now: You'll appreciate your chopped spinach salad with balsamic dressing so much more on a beautiful dinner plate. Invest in proper pots and pans to avoid chemicals that may be harmful; it may be more expen-sive now, but it will help protect the health of your family. Clean out your fridge and freezer every week *before* you go

grocery shopping. Keep a notebook with all of your family's favorite dinners in it: keep a list of ingredients at the top of the recipe/menu. This will save you so much time. Maybe choose themes for different nights of the week? (Italian, Barbecue, Chinese, Thai, Mexican, Comfort, Crockpot) You can find tons of ideas for your kitchen and menus on Pinterest. It's free and fun.

✳ **The entire house:** Take one day just to walk through your home and remove *clutter*. If your home is filled with too much stuff, it absolutely drains your *energy* and it's a dust magnet.

Simplify.

I know how sentimental your old doll or coffee mug collection can be to you. Maybe you could take an 'artistic' picture of it and display the picture beautifully somewhere; and then you could box it up and store it. *But honestly, what for?* I understand keeping memorabilia that is an investment and may be worth a fortune in the future. Perhaps you can set up a protected-display area for important collections that are valuable: Otherwise, sell it. You can use any profits to start a fund for a dream-vacation to Italy, or for your children and grandchildren's career-fund. What a smart remedy to help you avoid chaos in your home.

A simple home is classy and timeless. As I've gotten older, instead of turning into an inevitable hoarder, as older women often do (you wouldn't *believe* the cluttered homes I've seen), I've tried to be more simplified and streamlined, with less clutter sitting around, collecting dust. Let peaceful organization be the rule, instead of relying on dusty, old objects to meet your emotional needs. (Whoa, this is a whole other chapter I should have wrote.)

From the very first day we were married, one thing I've always tried to do was to treat each of our homes like it was the finest estate - even that shabby little apartment in Portland years ago. I've done my best to make our home look classy, simple and clean. I've painted many times myself, sewed curtains in a lot of our homes, I was always very careful with accessories, and just kept it as organized as I could with a husband and three sons. And we were flat-out broke for the first years of our marriage, so I know it doesn't take a lot of money to be simple and organized. It's free. And free is for me.

I knew a family that you would have been shocked to know they were actually living on welfare. They lived in a really cute apartment, but it was packed with stuff: the bedrooms were piled high with extra clothes on the floor and spilling out of the closets, the beds were unmade, their children's rooms were stuffed with brand new toys and the kitchen was packed with nonperishable food, stacked precariously on top of the fridge and cupboards. It was obvious that they had been blessed by many other 'angels' apart from me - which was amazing - but their atmosphere was out of order.

My heart was so sad, because they didn't realize that they alone were responsible for the *atmosphere of blessing* in their own home. I did help this sweet family, but I'm not sure if it made the impact that it could have.

Because, I truly believe that God does not tend to bless confusion; there's something powerful about *order*. Honestly, a clutter-free and organized home will do more to give you energy than buying the most expensive stuff in the world. Here's a principle that should impact you for the rest of your life:

**If you treat the things God has blessed you with,
with respect and gratefulness,
he will honor you and provide more
than you could ever imagine for your future.**

It's true and it works.

Speak Blessing

We just built a new home in Washington. While the house was still in the framing stage, Randy and I walked around and wrote scriptures of blessing in each room with black Sharpies. Godly words written into the very fiber of our atmosphere. Friends who visit often comment on the peace that they feel in our home:

Words kill, words give life,
They're either poison or fruit – you choose.
Proverbs 18:21 (TPT)

You might be thinking, *"Come on, writing words on your walls can influence the atmosphere of your home?"* Maybe they do, maybe they don't, but I'm certain the words that *'come out of our mouths'* do.

Just like I've shown you how *clutter* can influence your atmosphere, the *clutter* of toxic words will have the same affect.

Every word you speak over your life has consequences.

Years ago, Randy and I agreed with each other not to gossip or talk negatively about other people. Actually, Randy kind of made it a rule in our house, so I can't take credit for this brilliant decision. Of course, there are times when it's necessary to discuss or deal with problems and that's normal, but we both are careful to not gossip just for the fun of it. Gossip will come back and bite you – every time.

Did you know that gratefulness is the antidote for gossiping?

And I truly believe that a 'grateful heart' is a magnet for miracles. When you treat yourself and your home with an atmosphere of respect and gratefulness, you open up you and your family to blessings from God. I promise this works. It has for me over and over. Be grateful for what you have today and get the atmosphere in your home organized properly.

Now, you are ready to fine-tune your physical body.

Your Atmosphere - Your Body

＊ **Slow down:** One of the most important things I can get across to you in this chapter and throughout this book is that we all need to *slow down*. The false narrative that we need to always rush through our days or be in a hurry has caused untold damage to many of us. And it will probably take a long time for you to truly learn to slow down.

Start with meditating in the morning when you pray. Sit by yourself and connect with God.

Be intentional. Slow down your internal metronome. I've discovered over the last few years how incredible 'deep breathing' is for your health.

This *4/7/8 deep breathing method* is so good:

Exhale completely through your mouth, making a whoosh sound. Close your mouth and inhale quietly through your nose for 4 seconds. Hold your breath for 7 seconds. Exhale completely through your mouth for 8 seconds. Breathing in and out.

As I mentioned earlier, when I inhale, I always picture *'God filling me with his love or his peace or favor'*; whatever I need for that moment. I heard an expert say that slow, deep breathing six times in a row can help to change your entire mindset to a more positive outlook.

The benefits are endless, but it doesn't work if you hurry through and it doesn't work if you breathe shallowly. *Take deep, slow breaths.* Google the benefits of deep breathing, because it's incredible. Do it several times throughout the day, beginning in the morning. This will be your *foundation* for better eating and sleeping. It will.

Take moments throughout the day to just enjoy *being*. Snuggle with your children and read a book, enjoy a cup of coffee outside on the patio, walk barefoot on the grass in the sunshine, drink a cool glass of water and breathe deep, hold hands with your spouse while you talk about your dreams, belly laugh as much as you can, love on others, sit in a hot bath and close your eyes. Just *be*. This is what life is really about.

Slowing down.

* **Medical Health**: We need to take care of our body because it's a gift from God. And wouldn't we all want to be around to watch our grandkids change the world? Sit down and make appointments today for all of the medical tests that are necessary for someone 'your age'. (Ask your doctor or Google it) If you have any questions you're concerned about, make a list to take with you to your doctor. I've seen friends and family suffer needlessly with a chronic ailment or even a disease that

eventually took their life, simply because they didn't get the test in time. This includes your dentist, too. No excuses. Pick out a month of the year to take care of everything and put a reminder on your calendar.

Done. At least we can be proactive towards our health.

50 years old

❋ **Be grateful for the way God created you**: Remember I told you I was called *'Fatty Catty'* by someone when I was a little girl? That distorted image of myself has hummed on the *low burner* in the back of my head throughout my life. I've had to learn to speak back to myself each time I thought it and say out loud, "I reject the lies. I am in charge of my own health and well-being. I choose defiant love for myself and others. I am gratefully imperfect just the way God made me".

We are all privileged to take care of ourselves. If you're married, your husband will love it, too. My husband told me a long time ago, *"When you're healthy and confident, it frees me up to concentrate on being a leader for our family and loving you and our family the best I can".* A secret that many faithful, married men share is that they love it when their wives take care of themselves, exercise, eat better and hence; look healthier and feel more energetic as a result. Confidence is incredibly sexy. Do it for yourself first, but also for the ones you love. You were never made to be perfect, remember? *You are gratefully imperfect.* But when you are healthy and feel your best, it will enhance your intimate times and quality of life. It's a win-win situation.

Like I told you earlier, I have used food throughout my life as an emotional friend, but here's the amazing truth: Since I've been applying the tools in the previous chapters to heal my spiritual and mental life, *my eating habits and my diet have almost naturally adjusted themselves.*

So, if you need to refresh yourself on the previous chapters, go back and really absorb each chapter again; including the questions, prayers and listen to the worship music.

Each chapter is a *step* towards healing you from the inside out. Your physical body will naturally follow when your spiritual and emotional life is balanced with God. I believe it's the way he created us. To be balanced, begin with cleaning up your: Spiritual life, then your Mental life, and finally, your Physical life.

The biggest obstacle a lot of us face on the 'diet hamster wheel', is trying to work on our physical body *before* everything else. That's a big mistake and why most diets don't work in the long run.

✳ **The blessing of getting older**. You can enjoy being *gratefully imperfect* as you get older. We all get older. It's a lie from the enemy to make us feel like it's always better to be younger. Okay, we all had a blast and hopefully, we have some great memories from our younger years - but that's crap. Who died and declared it necessary to look like we're 29 for the rest of our lives? *(Hmm, I wonder who? Maybe the people who make billions off of our expensive skin creams, fillers and cosmetic surgeries?)*

I love the actress Jennifer Aniston's take on aging: *"I see women desperately trying to stay young, and my heart breaks...if you only knew how much older you look. They are trying to stop the clock and all you can see is an insecure person who won't let themselves age."*

The take-away? Ask for several opinions before you go in for Botox or fillers. I personally don't think there's anything wrong with that stuff and I've used a few different treatments, like Botox on the two lines between my eyebrows; but it's far better to remember *'less is most likely better than more'.* Really, there's something magnetic about a woman who is confident that God knew what he was doing when he created her and she knows her purpose for her life. She's not obnoxious or prideful, but she has a quiet confidence that she is living her life how God designed it for her. She rejects critical words about her exterior and sends love out to haters.

Doesn't that sound like a person you would like to be?

I actually feel better in my skin as I've gotten older.

I think of IKEA furniture when I think of trying to stay forever young on the outside. Let's be honest, a lot of their furniture is crap, with a capital C. It doesn't last. In the same way, no one in the world will stay 21 forever. Invest in the quality of your inner life. Get yourself balanced on the inside first and your exterior will soften and age gracefully.

Relax. Slow down and Breathe deep.
It's the small, slow steps
that add up
to the healthy person
you have the potential to become

Eating and exercise

(I am not a doctor or health professional. These are only sugges-
tions and some of the ways that I've enjoyed feeling better. Always
check with your doctor before you make any changes, especially if
you're pregnant or breastfeeding, have diabetes, or a history of buli-
mia or anorexia, or any eating disorder.) Here's a few hints for your
diet, but remember, t's really about what works for *you*.

* **Vitamins:** I don't want to get too technical with vitamins, because of course I'm not an expert, but here are some vitamins
that I take daily: A multivitamin and mineral supplement,
Vitamin D (in my opinion this could be one of the most important vitamins to take), fish oil supplement, Zinc, Vitamin
C, Calcium, Iron, and a prebiotic and probiotic. I will sometimes try new vitamins if I read about benefits that would suit
me at my age.

   I'm a huge fan of Vitamin D because of the extra protection it gives your immune system from infections, it's anti-in-
flammatory and helps protect your body from cancer. Another
great plus recently discovered? It helps reduce your appetite!
I'm not kidding. Oh, and one more proven benefit is that it
helps, (not a cure) protect you from the Coronavirus. (Google
it) I told you it was a rock star vitamin.

   (Check with your doctor for all vitamin dosage levels)

* **What We Eat and Drink:** One of the most important things
that you can do for your health, digestion, to lose weight and
to help keep your skin beautiful is to drink a lot of water. I'm
sure you're already aware of this amazing beverage, but this is
your friendly reminder to drink water early and often throughout the day. It's free and vital to your good health.

   I love to start my day with steel-cut oatmeal or scrambled
eggs and veggies. Oatmeal seems to fill me up and get my
digestion going for the day. But, whatever time that I do start
eating, I try to set a limit on the hours that I eat during the
day. Sometimes I skip breakfast if I'm not hungry. The latest
research has even proven that we don't always need to eat
breakfast. *Gulp*. Breakfast is necessary - for young children,

teenagers, pregnant and nursing women and if you're dealing with health issues - to provide fuel for their brain and for
their growing bodies. However, in most adults, studies have
shown that there are many benefits to intermittent fasting. In
addition to body weight, this kind of fasting can help lower
cholesterol, improve brain health and memory and a general
reduction in the risk of some diseases. Also, your fats that are
stored are more likely to be used as energy. It will take a few
weeks for your body to get used to this kind of a controlled
eating schedule, but the benefits are awesome.

If you want to eat healthy, I suggest a Mediterranean diet,
(Google it) and 8-hour rhythm fasting to help increase your
metabolism, and to help you stay healthier and live longer.
Don't skip the healthy protein – in fact, make sure to get
around 100 grams of protein a day, (there's 43 grams of protein in a chicken breast). Too many women, including me,
don't get enough protein and it leaves you *skinny fat*. I recently discovered that's one of the reasons why I struggle with
cellulite, (well, that and my crazy hormones). Our muscles
need *protein*.

I made a notebook years ago with my favorite recipes for
dinners, to help me avoid stress around dinnertime. Like I said
earlier, I suggest picking a different night of the week and let
it be a tradition for Italian food, or Chinese, or barbecue on
the grill, or Mediterranean or baked chicken or pot roast, or
maybe use the slow cooker one night. There's lots of ways to
get creative. Take one afternoon and print out pages of your
favorite recipes and put them in a notebook with plastic covers. I also tried the new meal kit companies that deliver to
your home for Randy when I was recovering from my jaw
surgery: It is so convenient, you can order as many nights as
you like, with as many servings as you need and they're surprisingly healthy and tasty.

Remember I told you that I planted a garden in Chapter 5?
I am so excited to enjoy fresh home-grown veggies this spring.
If it's possible, maybe you could grow your own vegetables?

Or you could at least plant some herbs on a window sill to start? At the grocery store, stick with organic as much as possible, including meat. And if you feel like it's too expensive, ask yourself if you can afford to spend money later in life on health issues like diabetes and obesity? Or if you can afford the difficult life-style of a body that is sluggish, overweight or sick?

But the other *incredible* benefit of being outside in a garden is to connect with the earth.

I'm serious. Just taking off your shoes and walking around on the grass in your backyard, or on the sand at the beach for an hour or two a day is incredibly beneficial for good health. It is a scientifically-researched practice with a number of health advantages, such as increasing antioxidants, reducing inflammation and improving sleep. Your kids need to play - from infancy on - in their bare feet outside. Drawing electrons from the earth improve our health, change the electrical activity in the brain, reduce stress and support immune function, regulate the nervous system, reduce cancer risk and help with weight management.

Basically, just get outside, (with sunscreen) as much as you can, walk barefoot and dig in the garden or even just play in the sand with your kids. Remember that Adam was created from the dirt? We are meant to connect with the earth *every day.*

If you *slow down* your rhythm, your metronome, and make the smart choices that I mention above, I believe you'll feel healthier than you've ever felt before.

Also, If I'm trying to lose any extra weight I may have put on from the holidays or from just living in the Pacific Northwest... I always remind myself that it takes *patience.* One of the hardest things I had to learn and still do come to terms with, is that eating healthy and waiting to see results *takes time.* Relax. *Slow down and breathe deep.*

It's the small, slow steps that add up to the healthy person you have the potential to become.

And your *energy* will soar.

✳ **Exercise:** I noticed an unusual phenomenon every time I go to Disneyland. Even though I eat more junk food than usual, I always wake up the next day a pound or two lighter.

It's the walking, guys.

Here's the easiest, healthiest and most beneficial exercise that almost anyone can do: Walk at a brisk pace, fast enough to work up a sweat, preferably on a slight incline, for an hour a day. There are too many health benefits to mention.

Remember to be nice to yourself with your exercise choice, because some people I know have had surgeries on their knees and shoulders at a somewhat young age. Be kind to your joints. I love kickboxing and group classes, as long as they're not too hard on my body. I am not great at yoga or Pilates, but I usually feel amazing after a class. (There's that *deep breathing* again).

I follow a health expert on Instagram - he has incredible results with his clients – and he says if you can *walk briskly an hour a day*, along with clean, protein-packed eating 80% of the time, drink lots of water and add light weights or body weight exercises a few times a week, this will help keep you on track to maintain a healthy life. Another reminder from him is that if you have a cheat day or week, it will usually take up to 7 'good eating and exercising' days to get you back on track. Be patient with yourself.

Remember to enjoy the miracle of music whenever you exercise, too. I love listening to my favorite playlists while working out or walking.

Celebrate God.
Sing together-everyone!
All you honest hearts, raise the roof!
Psalm 32:11 (MSG)

Woot, woot! Raise the roof!

✳ **Sleep:**

Nighty Night. The Holy Grail of your health is sleep. Sleep is imperative to a healthy body and sound mind. I still remember the night I brought my first little baby home from the hospital. I felt deliriously happy with our new little miracle, but the exhaustion I felt was *shocking*. I wasn't prepared for the mind-numbing fatigue that I was going to experience as a young mother. Sleep became a valuable commodity.

Throughout the years, I've never had an ongoing problem with sleep, thankfully, but as I've gotten older I've definitely struggled from time to time. Whatever the reason for losing sleep, I usually pay for any loss of sleep with grumpiness, overeating or looking and feeling exhausted. Because of the incredible benefit of sleep, it's important that you create an *atmosphere* for the best sleep possible. Take a look back on my bedroom ideas and here's a few other ideas to improve your sleep:

- Stop eating after 6 or 7 p.m. Limit your liquids so you're not up all night going to the bathroom.
- Turn off your phone and computer when it gets dark. Trust me - Google blue light. Charge your electronics in another room. This has helped me immensely.
- Take a warm shower or bath. Oh please, never go to sleep without one of these - for so many reasons.
- Keep your bedside table cleaned off.
- Use some kind of black out curtains or shades in your bedroom. Your body was made to sleep in very dark environments. Even cover your alarm clock, if possible.
- Use Melatonin or a calming decaffeinated tea before bed; don't drink any caffeine after 2 p.m.; or earlier, if it affects you too much.
- Aim to get 7 to 9 hours of sleep. Don't laugh! It's doable *(if you don't have babies, that is)* It's usually possible to go to bed earlier, right?

He that can take rest is greater than he that can take cities.
Benjamin Franklin

Doing this one day a week could change your life

I heard a story the other day that gave me chills.

During the Holocaust, the Jews kept the Sabbath, (a day to rest and honor God) as much as was humanly possible in the concentration camps. Whenever the Jewish prisoners kept the Sabbath and rested, they got their hope and spirit back, and they felt restored. The Nazi prison guards figured out that if they could disrupt their Sabbath ritual, through either taking food away so they were weak or many other ways, they could rob them of their spirit.

After the war, a journal was found written by a Nazi guard. In it, he had written, *"If we disturb the Sabbath of the Jews, they lose all their confidence and hope".* This is a chilling reminder to all of us of how much the health of your soul depends on rest.

In Japan, there's a word for dying from overworking or job-related exhaustion: *Karoshi.* People feel pressure to work 16+ hour days and even young workers are getting health issues, heart attacks or strokes, and tragically, many are committing suicide. It's called *death by overwork.*

Our bodies were not meant to keep going nonstop. To be clear, I'm not talking about nighttime sleep. I am talking about taking a Sabbath day, a day of rest *every single week.* Even God rested on the seventh day, after he had created the world and worked for six days. Not gonna' lie; if God did it, and actually *commanded* us to honor the Sabbath in the Ten Commandments, that's all the excuse I need. Absolutely no guilt.

Here are some ideas to help you learn to slow down and rest:

* Pick one day a week to *rest*. It doesn't have to be Sunday. If your day off is on Tuesday, take that day. Whatever works.

   Rest means to unplug. Unplug from technology. I know, I know, *"But this is impossible!"* No. It's not. Unless you're a surgeon and you're on call to perform open-heart surgery, you should be able to find one day a week to put down your phone and your computer. In fact, if you're on Facebook or

Instagram all the time and you're not stressed out or depressed, *how is that even possible?* Don't just sit vegging in front of the TV all day. Better yet, turn on some of your favorite music or the *Energy Playlist*, and change the atmosphere in your home.

✳ Set this day aside with your spouse or entire family, if possible. Make it a sacred day to reconnect with your *soul*. Take naps. Read a great book, with real pages. Play board games, (My husband and I have recently got back into Skip Bo and Monopoly. I'd love to play Scrabble, but I think he's a little intimidated by my 'linguistic prowess': *triple word score.)*

Take walks outside and sit down and have a picnic or play on the grass in your bare feet. Breathe deeply. Go out to dinner. Laugh together. Cook your favorite meal together. Even take a drive and look around at the scenic areas in your neck of the woods. Maybe take a 'dream drive' like my husband and I would do when we couldn't afford a beautiful home: We would drive around, dream and make plans for our future dream home. We have the best memories from those drives. Now we live close to the Columbia River in Washington and I love to walk across the *Bridge of the Gods* in the warmer (and drier) weather. It's stunning. (If you want to see it, it's at the end of the movie, *Wild,* when Reese Witherspoon walks out onto the bridge.) If you're in the city, do some research and find some safe public parks or grassy areas to enjoy. But even appreciating a beautiful sunset in your own backyard reminds you to slow down.

✳ If you want to use this day as a *de-cluttering* day and get organized, I think that's a fantastic idea; unless you have been overworked and haven't had a day off in a while. You'll know.

But honestly, it's sometimes more stressful to sit and look at the mess. If you do decide to make it a family day and organize, be sure and reward yourself and your family with a pizza party or dinner out, and maybe watch a movie together later. When you lay your head down at the end of the day, you can smile and know that you got rid of the clutter and improved your *atmosphere.*

* Most importantly, you can use your day to reconnect with God. He will refresh you. Little changes can heal big problems.

Confidence is sexy

You were made by God to feel sexy. The world has turned it into something dirty and I'm sick of giving them the authority to define what sexy is.

We were meant to be spunky and sexy. We were meant to feel good in our bodies. We're *gratefully imperfect,* remember?

My husband and I have made it routine for us to get away for a few days every three or four months. Since our boys were babies, we have taken a road trip somewhere a few hours away. This tradition has kept us communicating: you tend to open up about everything when you have time away. We've enjoyed laughing and having fun, but it was always a great time to reconnect intimately. Always! Nothing wrong with fun hotel time, right?

I can honestly say that these times away together have made our marriage happier, brought us closer and helped protect our relationship.

When we were poor and couldn't afford childcare, we'd either get our parents to help or we traded babysitting with other couples. There are lots of creative ways to find childcare. Save your change in a big jar? Stop buying Starbucks for a few months? It is 1000% worth it. And we still get away every 3 or 4 months. So, it's working.

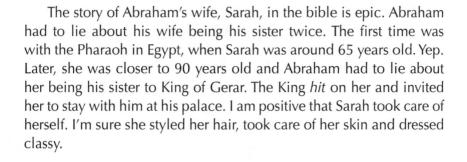

The story of Abraham's wife, Sarah, in the bible is epic. Abraham had to lie about his wife being his sister twice. The first time was with the Pharaoh in Egypt, when Sarah was around 65 years old. Yep. Later, she was closer to 90 years old and Abraham had to lie about her being his sister to King of Gerar. The King *hit* on her and invited her to stay with him at his palace. I am positive that Sarah took care of herself. I'm sure she styled her hair, took care of her skin and dressed classy.

I'm certain she was a hot number. I like to think she considered herself valuable enough at the age of 90 to continue to brim with Godly confidence of *grateful imperfection, radiance and beauty.*

Whether you are single or married, if you would adopt this God-confidence, you would walk differently and invest in yourself; and love yourself with *grateful imperfection.* Trust me. Confidence in God is magnetic. I've met people who may not have been considered the most attractive or in the best shape, but after watching their confidence and their joy, their *grateful imperfection,* they were stunning.

You are at your very best when you embrace everything you are. Accept yourself.

Breathe deep.

Be purposeful and *slow,* and keep going back over the steps in this book and this chapter until it becomes ingrained in you.

You are in control of your *atmosphere.*

And your atmosphere will be gorgeous.

Take Action:

1) What are some of the negative feelings and lies you strug-gle with from your past about your body? (Maybe something someone said or didn't say?)

   _____

   _____

   _____

2) What are some excuses that have been holding you back from a healthier and happier life? (i.e. I'm too fat, I'm not pretty enough, I'm too old...)

   _____

   _____

   _____

3) Have you had a wakeup call? _____ What was it or, more importantly, what would it take?

   _____

   _____

   _____

4) Name at least 5 things you love about your body and are grateful for:

   1.)
   2.)
   3.)
   4.)
   5.)

5) Name at least 5 things you love about your personality:

    1.)
    2.)
    3.)
    4.)
    5.)

6) Name 5 ways you can love on others to encourage them:

    1.)
    2.)
    3.)
    4.)
    5.)

7) What month will you schedule your physical tests and dentist appointments, and which tests do you need to schedule for your age?

_____

_____

_____

8) What is your favorite way to exercise?

_____

_____

_____

9) What are some ways you can make the atmosphere in your home amazing for your health and peace?

_____

_____

_____

10) What are some things big and small in your life that you're incredibly grateful for:

_____

_____

_____

11) Find a favorite verse that inspires you to live with excellence and to be 'gratefully imperfect'.

_____

_____

_____

Prayer:

Please say this prayer out loud

Dear Lord,

*Thank you for my home and the atmosphere that I am responsible for. I pray a hedge of protection around my house and my family. Help me to keep it uncluttered and organized so my family and I can enjoy peace and **just being**.*

*I am so grateful for this amazing body you have given me. I thank you for the chance to breathe deeply and move every day of my life. I confess that I have had negative feelings about myself, but, I am **gratefully imperfect**, and that's exactly the way I want to live.*

I choose to live a healthier and happier life starting today. Jesus is my healer and I declare today that every cell in my body is healthy and I will live a long life, fulfilled and love others to the best of my ability. Fill me with your energy right now. Fill me with your joy and give me a new excitement for life.

I am responsible for making the best decisions for my own health and confidence. No one else.

*Thank you for helping me create a **gorgeous atmosphere in my body and home**.*

In Jesus' name,
Amen

Energy Playlist:
Known

Energy Verses

...He never gets weary or worn out.
His intelligence is unlimited;
he is never puzzled over what to do!

He empowers the feeble
*and infuses the powerless with **increasing strength.***
Even young people faint and get exhausted;
But those who wait for God's grace.
will experience divine strength.
They will rise up on soaring wings and fly like eagles,
run their race without growing weary,
and walk through life without giving up.
Isaiah 40:28-31 (TPT)

For it is {not your strength, but it is} God who is effectively at work
*in you, both to will and to work {that is, strengthening, **energizing***
and creating in you the longing and the ability to fulfill your purpose}
for his good pleasure.
Philippians 2:13 (AMP)

*...And I find that the **strength of Christ's explosive power***
infuses me to conquer every difficulty.
Philippians 4:13 (TPT)

This is why I continue to toil and struggle -
because His amazing power and energy surge within me.
Colossians 1:29 (VOICE)

*...Be supernaturally **infused with strength** through your life-union with*
*the Lord Jesus. Stand victorious with the **force of his***
***explosive power** flowing in and through you.*
Ephesians 6:10 (TPT)

***Strength and dignity** are her clothing and her*
position is strong and secure;
And she smiles at the future
*{knowing that she and her family are **prepared**}.*
Proverbs 31:25 (AMP)

Energy is created in
an Atmosphere of Excellence

8

Rhythms of Grace

It is the Lord who directs your life,
for each step you take is ordained by God,
to bring you closer to your destiny.
So much of your life, then, remains a mystery.
Proverbs 20:24 (TPT)

We don't see things clearly.
We're squinting in a fog, peering through a mist.
But it won't be long before the weather clears
and the sun shines bright!
I Corinthians 13:12 (MSG)

I (Paul) ask God to make you intelligent and discerning in know-
ing him personally, your eyes focused and clear, so that you can see
exactly what it is he is calling you to do, grasp the immensity of this
glorious way of life he has for his followers,
*oh, the utter extravagance of his work in us who **trust him** –*
***endless energy**, boundless strength!*
Ephesians 1:16-19 (MSG)

I'm ready to trust God.

The females in my family are not gifted with navigation skills. Back in Ohio, we lived half an hour from the airport in Toledo and for years, a few of my female relatives would get lost on the way to the airport to pick up our Dad from a trip. Just so we're clear; that's a *30-minute straight drive on one freeway, guys*. Even today, the women in my family would be extremely nervous to drive in downtown Portland or on LA freeways, where I'm accustomed to driving. I might be one of the more gifted women in my family with directions, but I definitely need help sometimes, too.

Let me introduce you to my friend, Siri. I absolutely love using Siri to give me directions. How on earth did people get around in big cities before Siri or GPS? A friend told me that her dad still chooses to use the Thomas Guide when he's planning a trip. We all had a good laugh, but the truth is Siri isn't always right.

A few years ago, I was headed to do a walk-through on a house, and I had no idea where I was going, so I asked Siri for the directions. Since Siri sounded just as confident as usual, I followed her lead. The only problem was, Siri ended up directing me down this very long, very small dirt road which dead-ended at a cemetery, (*no pun intended*). At the end of the road, I turned my car around and came to a dead stop, (*that pun was intended*). Unless the homeowners lived in a cemetery, Siri had totally messed up the directions.

I dialed my husband, *"Randy, Siri took me to a cemetery, I'm going to be late to my appointment and it's a little creepy, too – help!"* After he stopped laughing, he gently scolded me for 'yet again' relying on Siri. You see, I've used Siri at different times when it was my job to 'navigate' our trips, and I've led him in the wrong direction more than a few of those times.

The moral of the story is: Siri is not perfect. And neither are you or I.

Proverbs 20:24 (TPT) tells us, *"It is the Lord who directs your life, for each step you take is ordained by God to bring you closer to your destiny. So much of your life, then, remains a mystery"*.

Believe it or not, that right there is beyond comforting to me.

If you're a follower of Jesus, he tells us that only he knows where we're going in this crazy life. And that we can trust him to lead us.

Welcome to God's plan, not yours

Jesus was preparing for the hardest thing he would ever do. He knew that being nailed to the cross was going to be unbelievably difficult, but he also knew it was part of his father God's plan of redemption for mankind and he was destined to follow God's plan.

He tried to explain it to his disciples, and Peter, *(dear, sweet, naïve Peter)* pulled him over to the side and said, *"No way, Lord. This is not going to happen!" (Peter thought he knew what was best – not a great decision.)*

But Jesus turned to him and said, *"Get behind me, Satan!" (I'm sure those words made the hairs on Peter's neck stand up.)*

"You are a stumbling block to Me; for you are not setting your mind on the things of God, but on things of men." Another translation says, *"You have no idea how God works".*

Could truer words be said?

Sometimes I feel like I'm sitting in a 3D movie without my cool glasses on. Everything is blurry and I'm trying to understand the story and predict what's going to happen, without getting a clear picture of the plot.

What's the bottom line? We don't know how God works:

We humans keep brainstorming options and plans,
but God's purpose prevails.
Proverbs 19:21 (MSG)

"For my thoughts are not your thoughts,
neither are my ways your ways",
declares the Lord. *"For as the heavens are higher than the earth, so are my ways higher than your ways and my thoughts higher than your thoughts."*
Isaiah 55:8-9 (AMP)

So, the million-dollar question is:
What is the best way to navigate your way through life, make the right choices, and stay on track with your purpose?

Choose to be childlike

In Mark 10, Jesus was sitting in a crowd, and some people were trying to bring their little children to be blessed and prayed for by Jesus. His disciples, once again thinking they knew what was best, tried to stop the people from bringing the kids to Jesus. They even scolded them. But Jesus was displeased with his disciples and said, *"Let the children come to me, for the Kingdom of God belongs to such as they. Don't send them away! I tell you as seriously as I know how that anyone who refuses to come to God as a little child will never be allowed into his Kingdom."* Mark 10:14-15 (TLB)

Yikes! Jesus is very, very clear.

God wants us to simply come to him as a *child*.

How do we come to God as a little child?

We choose to put our hope in God. We choose to be childlike, instead of cynical and we choose to trust. There's that 'T' word again.

What does it mean to be like a child? To me, it means:

> *Being open to learn,*
> *Trusting in God,*
> *Loving unconditionally,*
> *Laughing and being joyful,*
> *Sleeping peacefully,*
> *Eating a lot of ice cream, ('cause this is my own child-dream.)*
> *Forgiving and forgetting quickly,*
> *Learning every day,*
> *Growing,*
> *Dreaming,*
> *and loving life.*

What does it mean to *you* to *'be like a child'*?

Joy unleashed

When Randy and I were first married he told me that the only thing he could guarantee me is that I would never be bored and that our life would be an *adventure*.

And boy, was that true. Remember our dog, Hooper? The one who helped me get a separated shoulder? He fit into our adventure perfectly. Hooper was really a big toddler. A child.

He was always on the lookout for the next best thing. He loved everyone; I couldn't take him for a walk on the beach without him stopping and loving on everyone.

Speaking of leashes, he wasn't crazy about them and he was extremely strong-willed.

Hooper would escape to our sweet neighbor's house as much as he could, and they'd always bring him home with a big dog treat, every time - he was no dummy.

Hooper would chase skunks and come skulking back into the house, reeking from the skunk-spray – he had lots of baths.

When I cooked dinner, sometimes I'd put a big loaf of buttered French bread way back on the counter, turn around for a minute, turn back around, and it would be gone. Hooper always carried it outside and buried in the back yard – presumably to enjoy later.

He loved drinking water from the toilet.

He snuck onto my (forbidden) big living room chairs when I wasn't home – I know because the chairs would be covered with his golden hairs when I got home.

He didn't worry about much, because he could fall asleep in two seconds, anywhere, anytime.

He *loved* to hang his head out the window of the car while we were driving – even on the freeway.

He had a lot of friends on Facebook – especially for a dog who didn't belong to a celebrity.

He adored the ocean and any kind of water. In fact, I remember several years ago, our family lived on a cliff several hundred feet above the ocean. One day, my son was surfing with his friend, and as they turned on their boards to wait for the next wave, my son's friend asked, *"Dude, isn't that your dog?"* Hooper had escaped from the house, ran all the way down the crazy-steep, rough cliffside and swam out in the waves to hang out with the guys while they surfed. True story.

Hooper knew life was an adventure and he never wanted to miss out.

Just like, I repeat, *just like* the joy Hooper had, I believe God wants us to live with the same *unbridled joy*. God wants us to be like a child and let go. He wants us to laugh loudly, to enjoy our family and friends, to be spunky and fun, and to sleep peacefully.

When we totally depend on God, things will begin to change.

So even though we can be excited with life, look forward to fun times and be joyful, God wants us to always come back to him. To trust in the fact that he is a good God and He loves us and has a future planned for all of us. When we are convinced without a doubt that God loves us and he is always, always there for us, that's when our lives can really start to get fun. We are truly on an *adventure*, but we are secure in the knowledge that God is bigger than anything we will ever face for the rest of our lives. Period.

Just like Hooper needed a leash to help keep him out of harm's way and on the right path, because, let's face it, he was pretty crazy sometimes, we need hope in God as our connection to security and life. We can always come back to our salvation, to our forever *hope and trust* in a God who is always there, and we are confident that only God controls our future:

*This certain **hope** of being saved is a strong and trustworthy anchor for our souls, connecting us with God himself...*
Hebrews 6:19 (TLB)

I mentioned my sister, Becky, earlier. Becky has dealt with a lot of physical difficulties throughout her life. She was diagnosed with Multiple Sclerosis in her late 30's. She had to have her gall bladder and appendix removed. She was diagnosed with thyroid cancer and had surgery to remove a tumor and radiation for treatment. She faced a possible tumor in her uterus, that after another test, totally disappeared. She still deals with fatigue from the MS. But you know what? Through it all, she has maintained the most beautiful *hope*, in spite of the circumstances that have come her way. She's discovered that her hope lies in Christ and not the report from the doctor.

Last year, she had another scare: she was having severe pain in her stomach and had to go in for all kinds of tests. The last test she took ended up taking a few weeks to get back; and it was possible she might have cancer again. I thought she would be devastated and maybe say, *"You've got to be kidding me, God? Haven't I been through enough? How much more are you going to let happen to me?"*

I would have expected her to have a really bad attitude, because I know I probably would have – if I had gone through what she had to go through. But guess what?

She chose hope. She chose to believe that, *"By Jesus' stripes we are healed".* She chose *trust* and didn't let negative thoughts take over her mind. Throughout the two weeks she waited, I'd check in with her to see how she was doing, and I was constantly amazed at her cheerful attitude and total *trust* in God. She spoke with hope and positive faith. She told me she had given it all to God and she knew that she was going to be okay. It blew my mind.

Later that week, she went to the doctor and came skipping out of the office. *She had no cancer!* She had a small treatable irritation on her esophagus. She called and told me she was on cloud nine! Wouldn't you be? She is truly an example of hope.

If you have gotten a bad report, either physically or in any other way, I encourage you to look at the report through a lens of hope. Speak over the troubling news with positive words of hope and life. Use scripture to declare that *"By his stripes (wounds) we are healed",* Isaiah 53:5 (AMP) Look up scriptures that bring healing over your life, Google it or look them up in your own bible, and write them down. Declare them, speak them over yourself and the scary situation(s) every day of your life. Remember the power of your words. Remember the power of trust in God.

I believe that prayer and speaking over your life with hope changes things. I've seen it work in Becky's life, I saw it work in Tara's life from Chapter 6, and I've seen it work in my own life.

The Simple Life

One day last year, I noticed the lottery jackpot was enormous enough for me to shell out a few bucks; so, I pulled into a convenience store to get a bottle of water and buy some tickets. It was my turn in line and as I paid for my water, I asked the clerk for a few tickets, too. *"How much is the jackpot today?* I asked.

He smiled at me,
"It's up to $300 million dollars." Then he shook his head,
"You know, I don't want any of that money."
At that point, he had my full attention.
"What do you mean?"
"What would I do with it?" he said.
"The simple life is the best life, don't you think?"

I swallowed and nodded. I walked out to my car feeling silly for spending money on a notion that my life would be better if I had *more*. The cheerful clerk was right. *The simple life is the best life.*

It's not about accumulating more stuff.

No matter how rich you are, how beautiful and fit you are, how happy you are with your husband or wife or single - *the money will never fulfill you, your looks will never fulfill you, and a relationship with a husband, wife, boyfriend or girlfriend will never, ever be the answer to fulfillment.* Randy is pretty amazing and my sons are more than I could have ever dreamed to have as children, but they will never, ever fulfill the longing that I was created with.

The longing for a relationship with God.

Jani

I was leaving my gym the other day and Randy called to set a time to meet up later for dinner. While I was talking on my phone and pulling my car out of my parking space, I heard a knock on my window. Startled, I looked up to see a very old woman peering into my car. I honestly thought it was a homeless person and I tried to wave her away. There are a lot of homeless people in Portland, and while I've given some of them money, I felt nervous about this lady being a little more aggressive.

Then, I felt a tug on my heart. I told Randy to hold on for a second and rolled down my window to ask her how I could help her. She mumbled something and then she asked me if I could give her a ride. I knew immediately what I was supposed to do. *"Randy, I need to hang up, I'm going to give this lady a ride."* Randy wasn't happy with my decision, and he told me to be careful and to *watch out for a scam,* or something like that. I assured him I would call him the minute I dropped her off; and anyway, she was old and weighed about 95 pounds. I could defend myself if I needed to - those Body Pump classes were really paying off. So, I told her, *"Sure, I'll take you!"*, and I invited the sweet little lady to get in my car.

She told me her name was Jani, and she wore a raincoat with a multi-colored knit cap on her head and carried a bright red umbrella. Quite a character, from the looks of her. She asked me if I could drive her to her dentist appointment. *"Absolutely,"* I said and as I drove, she proceeded to tell me the sad and beautiful story of her life.

Jani had come to America from Scotland when she was 7 years old. She told me that when she was 25 years old, while she was studying to be a nurse, she went out on a date one night with an NFL football player. He ended up getting her drunk, (she had never drunk alcohol before), and brutally raped her. She said she woke up the next morning in a strange room; terrified. *Oh, dear Lord.* I asked her if she had called the police. No, she told me she was too ashamed to go to the hospital or to call the police, because she was so young and naïve.

She peered at me in my baseball cap and workout clothes and said, *"Young girls have to be careful. You look young - how old are you?"* I laughed and said she didn't need to worry, and that I was old enough to take care of myself. She went on with her story. She met a man few years later, and they were married for quite a long time, even though he cheated on her several times throughout their marriage. They ended up getting divorced after nearly twenty years of marriage.

She had four children: One of them died at the age of two and another died at seven years old. *I was afraid to ask how they died.* She had lived with one daughter for a long time, but that daughter had just kicked her out of the house; and now, Jani was on her own. She told me she had been staying at a hotel for the last month and a half.

I noticed she was having a little trouble talking and she told me she was having work done on her teeth. It seemed to me like she had a temporary set of dentures in and they kept slipping. In fact, she told me, I was driving her to another appointment with her dentist to fix her dentures.

She told me her social security check only paid her $2000 a month and that her hotel costs took up almost all of the money. *"Can you believe they would charge me that much?"* she asked, *"It all adds up."*

She pulled the bright cap off her head and told me her head had been shaved because she had slipped in the rain last week and hit her head hard on the pavement. Her soft gray hair was just beginning to grow back from the stitches. *"Are you okay?"* I asked. I mean, *how many more things could this poor lady go through?* Seriously. She told me her story in the span of about 15 minutes and I was blown away at everything she'd gone through.

I asked her if she knew Jesus and she said, *"Oh, yes, but I don't go to church very often."*

"You know, Jani, it's not just about going to church, it's about having a relationship with Jesus Christ and connecting with Him," I said, *"Are you close with God?"*

She nodded her head, *"Yes, I am. God is a big God, isn't He? He's brought me through so much".* No kidding.

We approached the spot where she wanted me to drop her off, and as I parked the car, I told her to wait a minute. It just so happened that I had withdrawn money from the bank that very morning to buy some furniture with, and I *knew* that I was supposed to give her more money than I usually gave to the less fortunate. As I pulled the money out of my wallet and tried to hand it to her, she saw the amount and refused to accept it. I pushed it into her hands and I tried every way I could to convince her to accept my gift. She refused.

She shook her head and said, *"No, that isn't why I asked you for a ride, I don't need your money."*

"Well, do you mind if I pray for you? I asked her.

"Oh, yes please!" she said. We closed our eyes together and I prayed over her life. I prayed for blessing and healing for her mouth and her injured head. I placed my hand on her shorn head as I prayed. After I finished, she squeezed my hand and told me *'Thank you'.*

She then told me she had a brother who lived in the Caribbean and her dream was to go live with him soon. I was startled because I was planning on going to the Caribbean next month, too. I told her where I was going on the cruise and she said that was where her brother lived. *What a coincidence.*

As she got out of the car, she asked me if I had kids.

"Yes, I have three boys and an amazing husband," I told her.

She said, *"He's a lucky man."*

"I'm the lucky one," I said.

She smiled and stared at me with her soft blue eyes and said,

"You and I are going to meet again, I just know it."

I gave her my name and number but I didn't ask for hers: I wish I would have. Jani told me three separate times while we were driving, *"You and I are going to meet again"*. Three times.

The hair stood up on my neck as I left her standing on the curb. She waved goodbye.

My phone rang and it was my husband calling to make sure I was okay. *"Randy, you aren't going to believe this lady's story."*

As I was driving back to the freeway, I looked down and realized that Jani had left her bright red umbrella on the floor of my car. *Oh no!* I remembered that she was staying at a hotel near my gym, so I drove over to the hotel and ran inside to drop the umbrella off.

"An elderly woman left this umbrella in my car; her name is Jani," I said, *"Do you know who she is?"*

The girl at the front desk had no idea. She directed me to another hotel across the street. I ran in and asked them if they knew who Jani was. They didn't either. Jani had said that she had been staying at one of these hotels for a month and a half? *Why didn't anyone know who she was?* I left the umbrella and described her to the person at the front desk to give it back to her if she came by.

And show hospitality to strangers, for they may be angels from God showing up as your guests.
Hebrew 13:2 (TPT)

Had I just been with an angel?

As I was driving home, I felt impressed that some of what this poor woman had been through had to do with what I had been writing about in this book. And then I had this thought: Maybe she was a mentally-challenged woman, and she had told me an elaborate, made-up story? After all, I am a pretty gullible person – not gonna' lie. But, then again, why didn't she accept the money I offered her? A lot of money. And there was no doubt, she carried herself with an aura of quiet grace. She was civil and centered. She didn't seem lost. Rather, love *oozed* from her. Whatever the truth was, this is how I chose to remember my encounter with sweet Jani: God was the one who allowed me to meet her. And maybe, who really knows for sure; some of the homeless souls that we meet *are* angels.

My perspective shifted.

I was so thankful to have met this amazing woman. One of the things that had the greatest impact on me was that she was still looking forward to beautiful days ahead, in spite of her hellish life so far. Her soft blue eyes were filled with *hope and childlike trust* and she was stunning.

When I got home, I ran to my computer to look up the meaning of the name *Jani,* (pronounced 'Yahnee'). I remembered that she was from Scotland, but her name was of Hebrew origin.

Jani meant *Gift from God.*

Whoever she was, or whatever her truth was, I truly believe God used her to speak to me in those few moments we were together. Even her teeth giving her trouble echoed the struggle I have had with my own teeth, on and off, all of my life.

But her hope showed me her *resiliency.*

I looked up the definition of resiliency and it means *the ability to mature, the ability to believe the storm will pass, the ability to thrive when others give up.* Jani was the epitome of *resilient hope.* She was still hanging onto the hope that God had birthed in her many years before.

Our souls are longing for a purpose and a reason to be alive.

Jani's life changed me. She had a purpose and God used her. She was meant to be alive for that special car ride and still much more. And I know that I am meant to be alive right this very moment, too.

As I mentioned earlier, my Mom had *three miscarriages* before she had me; and that was after having 4 other children. I was hit by a car while on my bike as a young girl, and walked away with barely a scratch. When I was a teenager, a car plowed into the back of the car my brother was driving; my friend, my brother and I were sitting in the front of the car and had any of us been in the back, one of us would have been crushed, (oh, and I had begged my brother to let me sit in the front). When I was newly married, I was blind-sided and my truck was totaled, yet not one scratch on my body. When I was a young mother, I was tossed in the air by a horse - I did a flip in the air and landed softly in the grass and I didn't have one broken bone - just a few sore muscles. I nearly drowned in the ocean while trying to swim out of a riptide. Looking back, I've had a lot of close calls.

It kind of gives me chills, in fact.

The point is, God clearly has a plan for me and he's not finished with me.

And God most definitely has a plan for you.

One of the things that had the greatest impact on me was that she was still looking forward to beautiful days ahead, in spite of her hellish life so far.
Her soft blue eyes were filled with hope and childlike trust and she was stunning

Destiny

But how do you know what your destiny or purpose for your life is? For many years, my husband has described the key to finding your destiny as: *Desire + Ability + Meeting a Need = Your Destiny or the*

Will of God.

First of all, it's never too late to *identify* your purpose. I think there are different points in your life when God gives you a chance to *pause* and re-access your talents, desires and creative ideas to love on others. Sometimes, it's time to say: *"Okay, I'm finished with 'this' – now it's time to move on."* Maybe you'll feel uncomfortable or excited or filled with faith. Everyone is different.

Or maybe you're already doing exactly what you were made to do. And that's amazing.

I have always loved to create. I've sewn the curtains in most of our homes over the years, painted and decorated all of our homes. I love to design and stage homes and I love to organize. But I've also been drawn to help young women over the years. I love spending time with both my young (and older friends); being a 'motherly influence', hanging out with them, praying with them when they make big and little decisions, and laughing with them as much as possible.

I'm not sure why these are the desires and abilities that God has given me, but I know that the *sum of my desires and abilities* are directing me toward the person that God wants me to be.

My love for organization inspired me to write this book about *energy* and organizing your life. I wanted to inspire others to get rid of the 'clutter' and organize their spiritual, mental and physical lives in a way that will create an atmosphere for energy. So, all the years that I was driven to organize our homes, all the years that I spent in small groups with younger girls listening to their pain and triumphs, all the years that I grew by walking through different situations and coming out stronger, God was preparing me for this step in my destiny. Because this book is just a step. Not the final destination. Just a step.

I encourage you to take a few days or however long you need to think about the direction that you believe God wants you to walk in. Remember, this means listening to your heart and its desires. *What do you love to do? What is it that comes easily to you? In what way do you feel like you would like to change the world for the better?* Are you naturally good at cooking? Are you a leader that people look up to? Do you love to draw and create art? Do you love children and enjoy teaching? Are you a musician or singer? Do you love entertaining people in your home? Are you a writer? Do you have a desire to start a new business or venture? Maybe you love traveling and reaching out to other people around the world? Do you love being a mom or dad and want to help parents learn how to raise their children with principles? There are a million and one talents that God has given to all of us.

And nobody can do what you do, like you do it.

I truly believe that if our lives are in tune with our destiny, whatever we decide to do will be beneficial for others, not just for ourselves.

So, when you sit down with a cup of tea or coffee and a gooey cinnamon roll for inspiration, make sure to do a few things -

 * Look up key verses in the Bible about wisdom and following the Lord's will. Go back over the incredible scriptures in every chapter of this book; all of them contain supernatural wisdom and empowerment.
 * Set aside time to pray and ask the Lord for direction.
 * Meditate and think about the abilities and talents that God has given to you.

You may need to ask others for ideas; sometimes, we have a warped view of ourselves and we're unable to see our strengths. Ask your spouse or a close friend. Often our parents will see things in us that we're unable to see. My parents have always commented on my love to create and saw the natural talents that I was born with. They always encouraged me to use them throughout my life and that meant so much to me.

Next, write a *life-mission statement*.

This statement should not be about your job choice or your career ambitions. The statement could be as simple as, *"I want to live a life that is focused on God and loving others. I want to give generously and live fearlessly to become the best version of me."* Feel free to borrow that one. Whatever statement you create, make it simple and write it down. Write it in this book, and print it out and hang it up somewhere to remind yourself of where you want the primary focus of your life to be directed. It is powerful.

And finally, write down the *next step* in your destiny. The step that I had to complete was writing this book back when I moved to Portland. *What do you believe is the next step for your life?*

**God will call you to do something that
you're already doing,
with a better attitude and a bigger purpose.**
Holly Furtick

Maybe it's time to try to adopt a child or try to have a baby with your spouse. Maybe you've been putting school off and it's time to sacrifice and finish your degree. My friend just finished her degree at the age of 61 - incredible. Maybe you need to consider looking for another job, because the job you have is not inspiring you or pushing you in the direction of your purpose. I'm not suggesting that you should quit your job, especially if you're not sure what you would do if you quit. Keep your job until you have the time and the clear head to plan.

But it doesn't cost anything to dream and plan, and God will help you determine your steps in your plan. If you take the time to listen and wait on His direction. Step by step.

I think the most important thing that I can get across to you is that your purpose doesn't have to be some 'grandiose thing' or that you have to be famous or that you have to make a lot of money. If you feel drawn to be an amazing waitress right now, that is exactly what you should do. Maybe you'll end up buying the restaurant you work in some day? Or if you love working with kids in daycare, do it with excellence. Love those beautiful children with all your heart and if you feel whole inside, you've hit the jackpot. And a lot of women are delighting in motherhood right now, and that is more than enough for them. I was a stay-at-home mother for years, and loved and valued the purpose that God gave me. (And mothers certainly meet a lot of needs, right?) But maybe it's not God's plan for you to be a mother; at least for right now. You can mother in many other capacities. Whenever I do returns at the Costco near my house, (which is a lot) I often talk with a woman that works in the return department. This lovely woman has impacted my life more than she will probably ever realize. She radiates kindness and love and I always walk away with a big smile on my face. She is using her gifts to make people feel loved. That's the definition of being a mother, to me. Find that special purpose that comes easy to you, that you love to do and that meets a need.

And connect with God. Stay close to him. Lean on God for direction and inspiration. Your purpose is doing what only you, ordained by God, can uniquely accomplish:

I (Paul) ask God to make you intelligent and discerning
in knowing him personally, your eyes focused and clear,
so that you can see exactly what it is he is calling you to do,
grasp the immensity of this glorious way of life he has for his followers,
*oh, the utter extravagance of his work in us who **trust** him –*
*endless **energy** boundless strength!*
Ephesians 1:16-19 (MSG)

God promises us *endless energy* when we follow our purpose. Oh, and did you notice the 'T' word again?
Trust God.

Balancing your life

I've spent most of this book talking about the importance of balance. *Balance* is one of the hardest things you will ever attempt to maintain in your life. Ask anyone.

The most successful people that I've met or even read about have often had to work hard at maintaining a balanced life. The reason I didn't focus in this book on your physical body as much is because I truly believe that if you don't start with the spiritual and get your personal relationship with Jesus Christ as the foundation of your life, everything else will be empty. Eventually. Your glossy looks will fade, your healthy body gets achy and older. Your friends leave you or get sick or will pass away. Your family is often more dysfunctional than perfect.

It's all about finding the balance where everything falls into place and *you can relax into the person God meant for you to be.*

If you still have things from your past that are bothering you, it's time to go back to Chapter 1 and keep working through it from the beginning to the end, until you are free. You might be forgetting something that is still upsetting your peace. *Forgiveness is letting go and moving on.* I still work on forgiving quickly and often.

If you struggle with fear, go back to Chapter 2 and speak the scriptures at the end of the chapter over and over your life. *Declare that God is light and there is no fear in God.* I still declare these scriptures often over my life.

If you feel weak, connect with God for power on a daily basis. Read Chapter 3 to be encouraged about *how much power we have when we connect and talk to God.* I will always connect with God, because I can't live without him.

If you feel unloved, start by loving others. Read Chapter 4 and keep loving those people that you see every day. *You'll find a deep empty hole being filled when you accept the love of Christ and love others.* I often breathe deep throughout my day and ask God to fill me with his love.

If you struggle with racing thoughts and you're too busy to think straight, review Chapter 5. We are in a battle every day for our minds. Period. *Taking control of your thoughts will take time, trust me, but if I can do it, you can, too.* I fight sometimes minute to minute to take control of my thoughts and it has changed my life forever. Fight for a sound mind.

If you were brought up in a dysfunctional family, like most of us were, re-read Chapter 6 and fight for a *supernatural breakthrough* in your family and yourself. Choose to be an Overcomer.

And in Chapter 7, create an 'atmosphere' for an organized and balanced home and body. You will feel peace. *You can breathe deep and know that you are in charge of creating a peaceful atmosphere. No one else.* I take time every single day to try to keep our home clean and organized and to take care of my body the best I can. I'm certainly not perfect; in fact, I'm *gratefully imperfect;* but it's incredibly empowering when you create a surrounding of peace and a clear space. You are in charge of your own gorgeous atmosphere.

So, maintaining a balanced life involves forgiving quickly, living with courage, being connected spiritually with God on a daily basis, loving yourself and others enormously, controlling your thoughts and schedule, refusing to let your emotions and dysfunctional upbringing control you, and following pretty simple, clean physical rules for your body and home.

If you want this book in a nutshell, I would say that's what *Energy* is about.

The Safe Place

Randy and I were in Idaho several years ago. We were with a friend and he was speaking at a large church. I was sitting back in the lobby, chatting with a few volunteers. All of the sudden I saw Randy race out of the main sanctuary, talking on his phone rather urgently. My immediate thoughts raced to one of my sons being hurt and my heart was pounding. I heard Randy say, *"I'll call you right back",* and he hung up the phone and grabbed my hand.

"What happened?" I asked.

Randy told me that one of our sons had been walking Hooper down the trail to the beach. Hooper, being the headstrong dog that he was, had gotten loose and run ahead of our son on the trail, racing to the ocean and excited to swim.

But poor Hooper didn't realize that a train was headed towards him. He barely beat the train and ended up on the opposite side of the tracks. Our son screamed *"Stay!",* but he didn't want to stay on the opposite side of the tracks without my son, so he tried to run ahead of the train. The powerful train hit Hooper on the head and he was catapulted to the side of the tracks.

Our son waited in anguish for the train to go by and when it passed, he ran to Hooper's side and pulled his broken, bleeding body into his arms.

Our son called my husband as Hooper took his last breath.

Hooper died. Our funny, child-like, adventurous dog.

And our hearts were broken. Randy and I left Idaho immediately and headed back to be with our family as quickly as possible. Our entire family came home that weekend and we sat sharing stories about our funny dog. We knew it wasn't anyone's fault that Hooper had gotten loose and hit by the train.In fact, we all kind of knew that something like this was going to happen to him some day - he was too exuberant, too headstrong and he didn't want to be controlled by a leash.

Hooper and my boys

The other day I was going through an old box of Christmas decorations.

I found Hooper's old leash in the bottom of the box. Funny that I would choose to keep something of Hooper's that he hated so much. Remember how he always yanked me around on our walks?

Hooper never understood that his leash was a necessary part of his life. That with his leash, he would be protected and go far more places with us than he would on his own, because *we knew* where it was safe for Hooper to walk. We were the ones who knew that we had to wait for the train to go by before crossing over to the ocean. His leash would have kept him from tragedy.

Just as Hooper would have been safe with the protection of his leash, in the same way, it is vital and life-sustaining to be connected to *Trust*.

God is always there. God protects, directs us and leads us on a path that he's prepared for us. He is our anchor, he is our connection, it is our *trust* in him that will sustain us through the good times and the bad times.

After all my talk about 'trust in God' throughout this book, I wanted to try to describe to you how it really feels when you finally learn to trust God over everything. Here it is.

You know that feeling of being head-over-heels in love and you feel like you are the happiest, most beautiful and unstoppable you've ever been?

That's it.

Trusting in God *completely* makes me feel like I'm loved, protected, desired, surrounded with favor and not worried about anything. When you're head-over-heels in love, the whole world hasn't changed - *you've changed.* You make the decision to let go, you make the decision to not be afraid, and you're excited to look ahead and believe 'miracles' will happen for you and your family in the future. You make the decision to allow God to meet your needs, not you. He knows better than you, what you truly need to feel loved.

You feel confident. You feel loved and beautiful. You don't let yourself compare your love with anyone else or your life with anyone else.

You are exploding with possibility.

That's how I feel when I'm in the 'comfort zone' of trusting God.

You let go of your life and anchor yourself to God. That is *trust in God.*

A glorious way to live

Last summer, Randy and I made a trip to our beautiful lake.

It was just the two of us; no echoes of our boys laughing or the rumble of the boat pulling them on their wakeboards. We took our jet ski and found a beach to sit on with a few chairs.

Towards the end of the day, I took the jet ski out and the water was glass and the evening sky was pink, just like it usually is.

Breathtaking and quiet.

Tears fell down my face as I said, *"Thank you for my life, God."*

I felt the most amazing connection with God. I was in my quiet place for real. After a few moments, I sped up to my usual turbo-speed, smiling and feeling young again. It was glorious.

Later, in the car as we were driving home, Randy looked over at me and said, *"I forgot to tell you something. You wouldn't believe what I saw while you were riding by on the jet ski."*

I stopped talking and stared at him.

"I saw a translucent-light figure sitting on your back, and then when you took off, it lifted up off of your shoulders. It was crazy-cool."

I had chills.

I may never know for sure if this was really an angelic being. Trust me, I don't have weird stuff happen to me like this. Like ever. *(Or, looking back at my life now, maybe I do?)* But, Randy has never seen anything like that before either; so I'm going to believe that it was God with me on the water.

Because this lake is my place where I come to get restored and God's in the business of restoration. I'm going to add this memory to my peaceful place, when I close my eyes and remember that *God is always with me*. He will never leave me.

Unforced Rhythms of Grace

This book is about finding *energy*. I've given you a formula that has worked magic in my life. You might ask, *"Come on, Cathy, magic?"*

Yes, *magic*.

God has a beautiful rhythm that he wants us to rest in.

God has the *exact plan* for your life. He does.

Like the ocean has waves. Like the seasons around us - rain, snow, storms, gentle breezes and sunshine. Like the seasons of your life – precious child, teen, young adult and beautiful woman (or man).

Life has a rhythm.

> *"Are you tired? Worn out? Burned out on religion?*
> *Come to me.*
> *Get away with me and you'll recover your life.*
> *I'll show you how to take a real rest.*
> *Walk with me and work with me - watch how I do it.*
> *Learn the **unforced rhythms of grace**.*
> *I won't lay anything heavy or ill-fitting on you.*

*Keep company with me and **you'll learn to live freely and lightly**."*
Matthew 11:28-30 (MSG)

That sounds like a beautiful poem, but it's scripture and it's Jesus describing to us how to slow down and live in the *unforced rhythms of grace. We can trust God with our future, because he's already there.*
Slow your metronome of busyness down. Trust God.
Breathe deep.
Stay connected to his energy.
Balanced and *gratefully imperfect.*
And may his favor be upon you for a thousand generations.
I love you, beautiful soul.
Energy is waiting for you.

Take Action:

1) What is the Mission Statement for your life?

   _____

   _____

   _____

2) What are some of the things you're naturally good at?

   _____

   _____

   _____

3) Do you believe you're headed in the right direction? _____
   What do you believe is the next step for your purpose, your
   destiny?

   _____

   _____

   _____

4) Choose a verse that inspires you to rest in the unforced
   rhythms of the grace of God.

   _____

   _____

   _____

Prayer:

Please say this prayer with me

Dear Father,
Thank you for the hope that I have in you.
All my hopes and dreams are founded in you.
No matter what I may go through today, tomorrow or fifty years from now, I know that I will always be connected to you, God, as my source of energy.

And my family will be blessed as a result of my choices.

Please show me my own personal mission statement for my life.
Help me to take the next step in my purpose today, and help me to plan for tomorrow.

I choose to stay close to you and look to you for direction.
Thank you for your energy.
I trust in you, always.

In Jesus' Name,
Amen

Energy Playlist:
The Blessing

Energy Scriptures

It is the Lord who directs your life,
for each step you take is ordained by God,
to bring you closer to your destiny.
So much of your life, then, remains a mystery.
Proverbs 20:24 (TPT)

I assure you and most solemnly say to you,
whoever does not receive the
Kingdom of God {with faith and humility}
like a child
will not enter it at all.
Luke 18:17 (AMP)

For I know the plans I have for you, says the Lord.
Plans to prosper you and not to harm you,
***plans to give you hope and a future**.*
Jeremiah 29:11 (NIV)

We don't see things clearly.
We're squinting in a fog, peering through a mist.
But it won't be long before the weather clears
and the sun shines bright!
I Corinthians 13:12 (MSG)

"Are you tired? Worn out? Burned out on religion?
Come to me. Get away with me and you'll recover your life.
*I'll show you how to take a **real rest**.*
Walk with me and work with me - watch how I do it.
*Learn the **unforced rhythms of grace**.*
I won't lay anything heavy or ill-fitting on you.
*Keep company with me and **you'll learn to live freely and lightly**."*
Matthew 11:28-30 (MSG)

*What a God! His road stretches **straight and smooth**.*
Every God-direction is road-tested.
Everyone who runs toward him
makes it.
Psalm 18:30 (MSG)

*And we pray that you would be **energized** with all of His*
explosive power *from the realm of his magnificent glory,*
*filling you with **great hope**.*
Colossians 1:11 (TPT)

Never doubt God's mighty power to work in you
and accomplish all this.
He will achieve infinitely more than
your greatest request, your most unbelievable dream,
and your wildest imagination!
He will outdo them all,
*For his miraculous power **constantly energizes** you.*
Ephesians 3:20 (TPT)

*Oh, the utter extravagance of his work in us who **<u>trust him</u>** -*
endless <u>energy</u>, boundless strength!
Ephesians 1:19 (MSG)

**Energy is trust
in the unforced rhythm of grace
from God**

66 Days to De-clutter Your Life

Creating an organized atmosphere starts with small steps. When we make small changes, over time, we will begin to see big changes. But it always starts with a *small change.*

I used to think that it took 21 days to adapt a new habit in your life, but researchers have discovered it actually takes at least 66 days, if not more. It's important to remember that it takes TIME to change or establish a habit.

I've stopped and started different habits and sometimes they have worked for me and sometimes they didn't work out. You'll know. The point of this exercise is to discover the habits that will create a simple life.

Below is a list of some small changes that each of us can start making. Choose one, choose a few, but just make sure to start small. Only choose the ones that will truly work in your life right now. Sometimes these changes will only be for a season in your life. The point is, each change is a step toward a more positive, fulfilled and ***Energetic Life.*** Check the habits in the list you would like to work on. It's best to start with one or two. Come back and try new habits as your Energy improves!

- ☐ Make time for devotions/personal prayer every day. Before you look at your phone.
- ☐ Set aside 5 minutes a few times a day for deep breathing and meditating on God. Use the 4/7/8 method: *Close your mouth and inhale quietly through your nose for 4 seconds.*

Hold your breath for 7 seconds. Exhale completely through your mouth for 8 seconds. Breathing in and out. While doing this, ask God to fill you with his love, energy, joy, peace, favor... make your own list.

☐ Write down your personal mission statement and put it up somewhere where you can look at it and read it every day.

☐ Make a plan for the next step in your purpose – Decide on incremental goals and the daily steps necessary that can bring you closer to your goal and purpose. (This is a personal choice)

☐ Continue to forgive. Pray for the people who may have hurt your feelings or who may even constantly annoy you. The more you pray for the offensive people, the more healing you will experience. Send them *love*. It works.

☐ Decide to cut down on Social Media if It's been stealing too much of your time. Set a daily time limit and stick with it.

☐ Be careful of the media and TV you are letting into your life. Be picky. It's subtle.

☐ Try to read sections of a positive, encouraging book every night before you go to sleep. Turn off the electronic devices two hours before bedtime. You will sleep so much better! Put your phone and computer in another room to charge.

☐ Write down 10 things every day that you are grateful for. Read them out loud both in the morning or before you go to sleep.

☐ If you are addicted to something, take a step every day toward cutting out that addiction. If it's junk food, get rid of all the junk out of your pantry and fridge. Decide you're going to just start making healthier choices by not ordering the fries, or even taking the bun off your In-N-Out Burger. Replace the junk with a healthier choice.

☐ If it's a serious or dangerous addiction, now is the time to GET HELP. Start today. Reach out to the appropriate professional for help.

☐ Maybe read Chapter 6 Restoration again: this is the *core reason* for many addictions. Take small steps and you'll be so glad you started. Also, go back to *trust in God*. Nothing else.

☐ Make it a point to encourage and say thank you to your spouse a few times a day. Keep it positive. When you're with your friends or in front of others, always build your partner up and even try to compliment them. It may sound silly, but they are your *biggest allies in life* and deserve to be loved and encouraged like they are the best person in the world – because they are to you. If It's your husband, show him respect as the Superman that he can be in your life. If it's your wife, love her extravagantly. Ask your mate what they would love to see and hear from you? What would mean the most?

☐ Plan a get-away with your spouse once every three months, even if it's just overnight. There are a million ways that you can do this – get creative. Start a get-away fund that you contribute your change to on a daily basis. Stop going to expensive coffee shops or pack your lunch instead of eating out. It adds up. Our marriage has stayed healthy and fun, in large part because of our quarterly get-aways.

☐ If you have children, plan for landmark times in their lives to discuss the Gospel and the *reason* your family serves the Lord. My husband took each of our sons away when they were 10 and then at the age of 16. He talked about age-appropriate issues. Help them understand the best way to live a moral life early on. Show them what happens when they make bad choices; the consequences. Before it's too late. Plan to spend 5 minutes a day *really listening* to your son or daughter. Kids need to be listened to.

If you won't listen and encourage them, they will look elsewhere.

☐ Try to exercise at least 5 times a week. Walk, hike, bike, go to the gym. Change it up, but start a habit to exercise. I still believe walking is GOLD.

☐ Make your yearly health checkup appointments. Determine the tests you may need for your age and schedule them. (This is a DEFINITE habit)

☐ Stretch. As we get older, our body loses flexibility. Try to stretch every day. If you do yoga or Pilates, that's great.

☐ Take time once a day to check in with your spouse. Really listen to each other during the day. Remind each other that you value them and you've got their back. Encourage them to dream. Talk about what each of you believe is the next step in your life purpose. Cheer them on!

☐ Find at least one person a day to smile at and encourage in some way. Give your time, your finances, a meal, a visit in the hospital or over coffee, take care of someone's kids overnight (the best) or even for a few hours to give them a break. Try paying for the person in front of you at the checkout line. They will be shocked. *It's awesome.*

☐ Read over the chapters in this book periodically; to determine if you're headed toward a more ENERGETIC life. Say no when you need to. Say yes to more (safe) adventures. Be courageous. Smile. Find the joy of where you are at this very moment in your life.

(Write some of your own habits to try)

_____

_____

_____

If you mess up, try again. And keep trying.
I love you.

Energy Playlist:
Forever and Amen

About the Author

Cathy Alward and her husband, Randy, own **Maranatha! Music**, a
fifty-year-old worship music company that reaches people around
the world and their real estate company,
*Creatus Properties/ **Ryan Schramm Real Estate**,*
in San Clemente, California.
Cathy loves anything to do with houses
and has designed, staged and flipped houses
throughout her life –
emphasizing simplicity and excellence.
Cathy's led small groups, with a focus on mentoring young
women, and has also been honored to speak in front of
women's groups and churches.
She loves to connect with women of all ages.
Cathy, and Randy, her husband of over 37 years, divide their time
between Washington and Southern California,
to visit their 3 grown-sons' families,
and their beautiful grandchildren.
She is excited to 'dig the weeds' out of her garden this spring,
and to welcome some new chickens to their property.

Connect
Website: www.cathyalward.com
(detailed contact info found on the site)
Instagram: @cathy.alward
Facebook: www.Facebook.com/cathyjalward

Thank you to my beautiful family
for your loving support -
especially my brilliant husband, Randy.
Thank you to Merrilee Hauser
for your editing talents.
Thank you to
my agent, Linda Klosterman,
Adam Smucker, Stan Sinclair
and Jim Rasfeld –
The best team ever.

CPSIA information can be obtained
at www.ICGtesting.com
Printed in the USA
FSHW010245090521
81195FS